OCR GCSE

Religious Studies B
Philosophy & Applied Ethics

Christian Philosophy & Applied Ethics

Vicky Bunting · Janet Dyson · Tanya Hill
Gordon Kay · Ina Taylor · Cavan Wood

Series editor: Janet Dyson
Series consultant: Jon Mayled

www.heinemann.co.uk

✓ Free online support
✓ Useful weblinks
✓ 24 hour online ordering

01865 888080

OCR AND HEINEMANN ARE WORKING TOGETHER TO PROVIDE BETTER SUPPORT FOR YOU

Official Publisher Partnership

Pearson Education Limited is a company incorporated in England and Wales, having its registered office at Edinburgh Gate, Harlow, Essex, CM20 2JE. Registered company number: 872828

www.pearsonschoolsandfecolleges.co.uk

Limited Text © Pearson Education Limited 2009

First published 2009

15
10 9 8 7

British Library Cataloguing in Publication Data
A catalogue record for this book is available from the British Library

ISBN 978-0-435-50158-7

Edited by Bruce Nicholson
Reviewed by Richard Gray
Proofread by Tracey Smith
Project managed and typeset by Wearset Ltd,
Boldon, Tyne and Wear
Original illustrations © Pearson Education Limited 2009
Illustrated by Chris Coady and Wearset Ltd
Picture research by Q2AMedia
Cover illustration © Petrovich 9/iStockphoto
Printed in China (CTPS/07)

Acknowledgements
The authors and publisher would like to thank the following individuals and organisations for permission to reproduce photographs:

Page 6 Kirill Volkov/Shutterstock. Page 7 INTERFOTO Pressebildagentur/Alamy. Page 8 Mary Evans Picture Library. Page 10 Associated Press. Page 11 scenicireland.com/ Christopher Hill Photographic/Alamy. Page 16 Kimber Rey Solana/Shutterstock. Page 18 Pearson Education Ltd. Tudor Photography. Page 24 Liz Van Steenburgh/Shutterstock. Page 30 Rob Griffith/Associated Press. Page 32 Velora/Shutterstock. Page 34 Michelangelo (1475–1564)/Vatican Museums and Galleries, Vatican City, Italy/The Bridgeman Art Library. Page 38 Pixonnet.com/Alamy. Page 39 Kenneth Sponsler/ Dreamstime. Page 46 Dom Holdsworth. Page Sygma/Corbis. Page 48 BananaStock/Jupiter Images. Page 47 Masaccio, Tommaso (1401–28) Brancacci Chapel, Santa Maria del Carmine, Florence, Italy/The Bridgeman Art Library. Page 50 The London Art Archive/Alamy. Page 38 Pixonnet.com/Alamy. Page 39 Kenneth Sponsler/Dreamstime. Page 46 Dom Holdsworth. Page Sygma/Corbis. Page 48 BananaStock/Jupiter Images. Page 47 Masaccio, Tommaso (1401–28) Brancacci Chapel, Santa Maria del Carmine, Florence, Italy/The Bridgeman Art Library. Page 50 The London Art Archive/ Alamy. Page 45 Nick Ut/Associated Press. Page 59 Serg64/ Shutterstock. Page 60 Stefano Bianchetti/Corbis. Page 62 Dr_Flash/Shutterstock. Page 66 Archive/CSA Images/Corbis. Page 78 Pearson Education Ltd. Lord and Leverett. Page 96 Image Source/Jupiter Images. Page 98 LondonPhotos – Homer Sykes/Alamy. Page 100 Pascal Genest/Istockphoto. Page 102 Chris Young/Associated Press. Page 105 Jason Burtt/ Silverringthings. Page 110 Tom Stewart/Corbis. Page 112 Dr Najeeb Layyous/Science Photo Library. Page 115 Content Mine International/Alamy. Page 117 Caters News Agency Ltd/ Rex Features. Page 126 Mohsin Raza/Reuters. Page 129 ImageState/Alamy. Page 130 Rob Griffith/Associated Press. Page 132 Andresr/Shutterstock. Page 134 Toby Melville/ Reuters. Page 138 Stephen Meese/Shutterstock. Page 140 Nabil Al-Jurani/Associated Press. Page 144 Lou Oates/Shutterstock. Page 152 Nyul/Fotolia. Page 154 Hulton Archive/Getty Images. Page 156 Andresr/Shutterstock. Page 157 LondonPhotos – Homer Sykes/Alamy. Page 159 Arcaid/Alamy. Page 160 Richard Klune/Corbis. Page 166 kwest/Shutterstock. Page 170 KPA Honorar&Belege. Page 173 Rex Features. Page 174 Nils Jorgensen/Rex Features.

The authors and publisher would like to thank the following for permission to use copyright material:

Contents

Introduction

A note for teachers

This student book has been written especially to support the Christianity sections of the OCR Religious Studies Specification B Philosophy and/or Applied Ethics. The specification is composed of four Units – B601: *Philosophy 1 (Belief about deity; Religious and spiritual experience; The end of life)*, B602: *Philosophy 2 (Good and evil; Religion, reason and revelation; Religion and science)*, B603: *Ethics 1 (Religion and human relationships; Religion and medical ethics; Religion, poverty and wealth)*, B604: *Ethics 2 (Religion, peace and justice; Religion and equality; Religion and the media)*. This book is part of an overall series covering the OCR Specification B, which comprises:

- three Student Books: one on Philosophy, covering all six religions in the specification; one on Applied Ethics, also covering all six religions; and this book – further details on pages viii and ix

- a Teacher Guide covering Buddhism, Christianity, Hinduism, Islam, Judaism and Sikhism – further details on pages viii and ix.

Who are we?

The people who have planned and contributed to this series of books include teachers, advisers, inspectors, teacher trainers and GCSE examiners, all of whom have specialist knowledge of Religious Studies. For all of us the subject has a real fascination and we believe that good Religious Studies can make a major contribution to developing the skills, insights and understanding people need in today's world. In the initial development of this series, Pamela Draycott lent us her expertise, which we gratefully acknowledge.

Why is Religious Studies an important subject?

We believe that Religious Studies is an important subject because every area of life is touched by issues to do with religion and belief. Following a Religious Studies GCSE course will enable students to study and explore what people believe about God, authority, worship, beliefs, values and truth. Students will have opportunities to engage with questions about why people believe in God and how beliefs can influence many aspects of their lives.

Students will also explore why members of a particular religion may believe different things. In lessons students will be expected to think, talk, discuss, question and challenge, reflect on and assess a wide range of questions. As young people growing up in a diverse society studying religion will help them to understand and relate to people whose beliefs, values and viewpoints differ from their own, and help them to deal with issues arising, not only in school, but in the community and workplace.

The study of religion will also help students to make connections with a whole range of other important areas, such as music, literature, art, politics, economics and social issues.

The specification for OCR B Philosophy and/or Applied Ethics

The specification outlines the aims and purposes of GCSE. The content to be covered is divided into twelve different Topics, three for each of the four Units. The book's structure follows these Topic divisions precisely:

Unit B601: Philosophy 1

Topic 1: Belief about deity

Topic 2: Religious and spiritual experience

Topic 3: The end of life

Unit B602: Philosophy 2

Topic 1: Good and evil

Topic 2: Religion, reason and revelation

Topic 3: Religion and science

Unit B603: Ethics 1

Topic 1: Religion and human relationships

Topic 2: Religion and medical ethics

Topic 3: Religion, poverty and wealth

Unit B604: Ethics 2

Topic 1: Religion, peace and justice

Topic 2: Religion and equality

Topic 3: Religion and the media

The Topics focus on developing skills such as analysis, empathy and evaluation, which will enable students to gain knowledge and understanding of the specified content.

In following this specification students will have the opportunity to study Philosophy and/or Applied Ethics in depth and will learn about Christianity's diversity and the way in which people who believe it follow its teachings in their everyday lives.

This book covers everything students will need to know for the examination and shows them how to use their knowledge and understanding to answer the questions they will be asked.

Why did we want to write these resources?

We feel strongly that there is a need for good classroom resources which:

- make the subject lively, interactive and relevant to today's world
- encourage students to talk to each other and work together
- challenge students and encourage them to think in depth in order to reach a high level of critical thinking
- train students to organise their thoughts in writing in a persuasive and structured way, and so prepare them for examination

The book has many features which contribute towards these goals. **Grade Studio** provides stimulating and realistic exercises to train students in what examiners are looking for and how to meet those expectations. **Exam Café** provides an exciting environment in which students can plan and carry out their revision.

Of course learning is about more than just exams. Throughout the book you will find **Research Notes**, which encourage students to explore beyond the book and beyond the curriculum. All of these features are explained in more detail on the next two pages.

What is in this book?

This student book has the following sections:

- the **Introduction**, which you are reading now
- the twelve **Topics** covered in the specification
- **Exam Café** – an invaluable resource for students studying their GCSE in Religious Studies
- **Glossary** – a reference tool for key terms and words used throughout the book.

Each of the above is covered in more detail in the text below.

The twelve Topics

Each Topic in this book contains:

- a Topic scene-setter which looks at the key questions raised by the Topic, and the key words associated with those questions (**The Big Picture**)
- two-page spreads covering the **main Topic content**
- two pages of different level questions to check understanding of the Topic material (**Remember and Reflect**)
- exam-style questions with level indicators, examiner's comments and model answers (**Grade Studio**).

These features, which are explained more fully in the following pages, have been carefully planned and designed to draw together the OCR specification in an exciting but manageable way.

The Big Picture

This provides an overview of the Topic. It presents the requirements of the specification in a student friendly way. It includes a section, **Did you know?**, which offers a selection of thought-provoking, often surprising facts

and observations from the Topic's contents, designed to engage and excite students about the content. This is followed by a useful reference list of **Key Words**. Finally, there is a **Get started** activity, often linked to a picture or visual stimulus, which presents a task also designed to engage students in the issues.

Main Topic content

The main content of each Topic is covered in a number of two-page spreads. Each spread equates to roughly one lesson of work – although teachers will need to judge for themselves if some of these need more time.

Each spread begins with the learning outcomes, highlighted in a box at the top of the page, so that students are aware of the focus and aims of the lesson. The text then attempts to answer, through a balanced viewpoint, one or two of the key questions raised in **Did you know?**. The text carefully covers the views of both religious believers and non-believers. It is also punctuated with activities that range from simple tasks that can take place in the classroom to more complex tasks that can be tackled away from school.

A range of margin features adds extra depth and support to the main text both for students and the teacher.

- **For debate** invites students to examine two sides of a controversial issue.
- **Must think about!** directs students towards a key idea that they should consider.
- **Sacred text** provides an extract from Christian sacred texts covered in the Topic to help students understand religious ideas and teachings.

- **Research notes** provide stimulating ideas for further research beyond the material covered in the book and in the OCR specification.

Activities

Every Topic has a range of interesting activities which will help students to achieve the learning outcomes. Every two-page spread has a short starter activity to grab students' attention and to get them thinking. This is followed by a development section where the main content is introduced, and a plenary activity, which may ask students to reflect on what they have learnt, or may start them thinking about the next steps.

All activities are labelled **AO1** or **AO2** so you can tell at a glance which skills will be developed.

Remember and Reflect

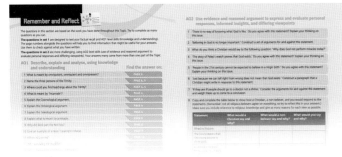

This provides an opportunity for students to reflect on what they have learned and identify possible weaknesses or gaps in their knowledge. It also helps them to recognise key ideas in the specification content. Once they have tested their knowledge with the first set of questions, a cross-reference takes them back to the relevant part of the text so they can check their answers. A second set of questions helps them to develop the AO2 skills necessary for the examination.

What is Grade Studio?

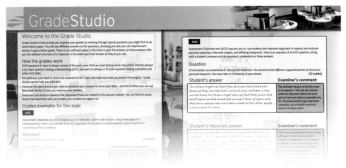

Everyone has different learning needs and this section of the book gives clear focus on how, with guidance from the teacher, students can develop the skills that will help them to achieve the higher levels in their exam responses.

Grade Studio appears as a two-page spread at the end of every Topic. It includes tips from the examiner, guidance on the steps to completing a well-structured answer, and sample answers with examiner comments.

What is the Exam Café?

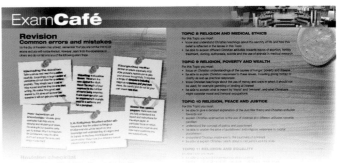

This is the revision section of the book. Here students will find useful revision tools and tips on how to get started on their revision and exam preparation. Students will also find assessment advice, including examples of different types of questions and samples of frequently asked questions. A useful **revision check list** allows students to review each Topic's content and explains where to find material in the book that relates to the exam questions.

Exam Café also has:

- sample student answers with comments
- help on understanding exam language, so students can achieve higher grades
- tips, including common mistakes to be avoided.

Heinemann's Religious Studies B OCR Series

Below is a snapshot of the complete OCR Religious Studies B series. Further detail can be found at www.pearsonschoolsandfecolleges.co.uk

OCR B Philosophy and Applied Ethics Teacher Guide with editable CD-ROM

ISBN 978-0-435-50152-5

The Teacher Guide has been designed to correspond closely to the Student Book. For every Topic, the Teacher Guide offers four sample lesson plans and worksheets on Christianity, as well as a two page **Grade Studio**. There is careful cross-referencing throughout to help Teachers make the most out of these resources. In addition, the Teacher Guide contains one sample lesson plan per Topic for Buddhism, Hinduism, Islam, Judaism and Sikhism.

Finally, the Teacher Guide comes with an **editable CD-ROM**, which contains all the lesson plans along with a fully customisable version of all the worksheets.

Philosophy Student Book with ActiveBook CD-ROM

ISBN 978-0-435-50150-1

This book provides complete coverage of both units of Philosophy (B601 and B602) and covers all six religions: Buddhism, Christianity, Hinduism, Islam, Judaism and Sikhism. It provides information, activities, and Grade Studio examples for all aspects of the course, as well as an eight-page **Exam Café** for revision. Each book comes with an **ActiveBook CD-ROM. ActiveBook** contains an electronic version of the Student Book, as well as an exciting, electronic Exam Café, which offers fresh revision content, complementing and extending the Exam Café in the book itself.

For the Teacher, the book is fully supported by the **OCR B Teacher Guide** (see above) and by the **Philosophy ActiveTeach CD-ROM** (see below).

Philosophy
ActiveTeach CD-ROM
ISBN 978-0-435-50155-6

The **ActiveTeach CD-ROM** contains an electronic version of the **Philosophy Student Book**, along with interactive **Grade Studio** and interactive whiteboard activities for front-of-class teaching. These activities are invaluable in engaging students with the specification content and bringing religious debates and issues to life. Equally valuable are the video and audio clips offered throughout the content. ActiveTeach has a special **zoom feature**, so any part of the book's content can be expanded on the whiteboard, as well as a special **My Resources** feature, where favourite activities, pages or clips can be stored. Finally, ActiveTeach includes an electronic **Exam Café**, which offers fresh revision content, complementing and extending the Exam Café in the book itself. A VLE version of ActiveTeach is available at no extra cost.

Applied Ethics
ActiveTeach CD-ROM
ISBN 978-0-435-50156-3

The **ActiveTeach CD-ROM** contains an electronic version of the **Applied Ethics Student Book**, along with interactive **Grade Studio** and interactive whiteboard activities for front-of-class teaching. These activities are invaluable in engaging students with the specification content and bringing religious debates and issues to life. Equally valuable are the video and audio clips offered throughout the content. ActiveTeach has a special **zoom feature**, so any part of the book's content can be expanded on the whiteboard, as well as a special **My Resources** feature, where favourite activities, pages or clips can be stored. Finally, ActiveTeach includes an electronic **Exam Café**, which offers fresh revision content, complementing and extending the Exam Café in the book itself. A VLE version of ActiveTeach is available at no extra cost.

Applied Ethics
Student Book with
ActiveBook CD-ROM
ISBN 978-0-435-50151-8

This book provides complete coverage of both units of Applied Ethics (B603 and B604) and covers all six religions: Buddhism, Christianity, Hinduism, Islam, Judaism and Sikhism. It provides information, activities, and **Grade Studio** examples for all aspects of the course, as well as an 8-page **Exam Café** for revision. Each book comes with an **ActiveBook CD-ROM.** ActiveBook contains an electronic version of the **Student Book**, as well as an exciting, electronic Exam Café, which offers fresh revision content, complementing and extending the Exam Café in the book itself.

For the Teacher, the book is fully supported by the **OCR B Teacher Guide** (see above) and by the **Applied Ethics ActiveTeach CD-ROM** (see below).

Assessment Objectives and Levels of Response

Assessment Objectives, AO1 and AO2

In the specification, the questions in the examination are designed to test students against two Assessment Objectives: AO1 and AO2. In the specification 50 per cent of the marks will be awarded for AO1 questions and 50 per cent will be awarded for AO2 questions.

AO1 Questions require candidates to 'describe, explain and analyse, using knowledge and understanding'.

AO2 Questions require candidates to 'use evidence and reasoned argument to express and evaluate personal responses, informed insights, and differing viewpoints'.

Each question in the examination is composed of 5 parts, **a–e**. In more detail:

- Parts **a–c** are worth one, two and three marks respectively and test a candidate's knowledge (AO1 skills).
- Part **d** is worth six marks and tests a candidate's understanding (AO1 skills).
- Part **e** is worth twelve marks and tests a candidate's AO2 skills.

From **January 2013**, all of the units will carry additional marks for spelling, punctuation and grammar. The question where these marks apply will be marked with a pencil icon.

LEVELS OF RESPONSE FOR MARKING AO1 PART (D) QUESTIONS

LEVEL 1
(1–2 marks)

A **weak** attempt to answer the question.

Candidates will demonstrate little understanding of the question.

- A small amount of relevant information may be included.
- Answers may be in the form of a list with little or no description/explanation/analysis.
- There will be little or no use of specialist terms.
- Answers may be ambiguous or disorganised.
- Errors of grammar, punctuation and spelling may be intrusive.

LEVEL 2
(3–4 marks)

A **satisfactory** answer to the question.

Candidates will demonstrate some understanding of the question.

- Information will be relevant but may lack specific detail.
- There will be some description/explanation/analysis although this may not be fully developed.
- The information will be presented for the most part in a structured format.
- Some use of specialist terms, although these may not always be used appropriately.
- There may be errors in spelling, grammar and punctuation.

LEVEL 3
(5–6 marks)

A **good** answer to the question.

Candidates will demonstrate a clear understanding of the question.

- A fairly complete and full description/explanation/analysis.
- A comprehensive account of the range and depth of relevant material.
- The information will be presented in a structured format.
- There will be significant, appropriate and correct use of specialist terms.
- There will be few, if any, errors in spelling, grammar and punctuation.

LEVELS OF RESPONSE FOR MARKING AO2 PART (E) QUESTIONS

LEVEL 0

(0 marks)

No evidence submitted or response does not address the question.

LEVEL 1

(1–3 marks)

A **weak** attempt to answer the question.

Candidates will demonstrate little understanding of the question.

- Answers may be simplistic with little or no relevant information.
- Viewpoints may not be supported or appropriate.
- Answers may be ambiguous or disorganised.
- There will be little or no use of specialist terms.
- Errors of grammar, punctuation and spelling may be intrusive.

LEVEL 2

(4–6 marks)

A **limited** answer to the question.

Candidates will demonstrate some understanding of the question.

- Some information will be relevant, although may lack specific detail.
- Only one view might be offered and developed.
- Viewpoints might be stated and supported with limited argument/discussion.
- The information will show some organisation.
- Reference to the religion studied may be vague.
- Some use of specialist terms, although these may not always be used appropriately.
- There may be errors in spelling, grammar and punctuation.

LEVEL 3

(7–9 marks)

A **competent** answer to the question.

Candidates will demonstrate a sound understanding of the question.

- Selection of relevant material with appropriate development.
- Evidence of appropriate personal response.
- Justified arguments/different points of view supported by some discussion.
- The information will be presented in a structured format.
- Some appropriate reference to the religion studied.
- Specialist terms will be used appropriately and for the most part correctly.
- There may be occasional errors in spelling, grammar and punctuation.

LEVEL 4

(10–12 marks)

A **good** answer to the question.

Candidates will demonstrate a clear understanding of the question.

- Answers will reflect the significance of the issue(s) raised.
- Clear evidence of an appropriate personal response, fully supported.
- A range of points of view supported by justified arguments/discussion.
- The information will be presented in a clear and organised way.
- Clear reference to the religion studied.
- Specialist terms will be used appropriately and correctly.
- Few, if any, errors in spelling, grammar and punctuation.

Topic 1: Belief about deity

The Big Picture

In this Topic, you will be addressing Christian beliefs and teachings about:

- the nature of God
- reasons for belief in God
- the concept of miracles
- the ways in which these beliefs affect the life and outlook of Christians in the world today.

You will also think about your own feelings and responses to these questions and issues.

DID YOU KNOW?

- Christians believe there is only one God (monotheism), who is omnipotent and omniscient. Their God is a loving God and cares how people behave and treat each other. They believe in the doctrine of the Trinity, which shows that God can be understood in three different ways – as Father, Son and Holy Spirit.

- Christians believe God designed and created the universe and that God has a purpose for humanity.

- Christians experience God in many different ways and communicate with him through prayer.

- Christians believe the most important example of God's intervention in the world was in God taking human form as his son, Jesus, known as the incarnation.

- They believe God is active in the world and performs miracles such as healing the sick.

Apostles' Creed An early statement of Christian belief.

Cosmological argument The argument that there must be a 'first cause' and that this was God.

Father One person of the threefold nature of God.

forgiveness The teaching of forgiveness forms part of the most important and widely used Christian prayer – the prayer Jesus taught his disciples, commonly known as the Lord's Prayer.

Heaven A Christian idea of paradise where the soul goes after death if it is free from sin to have eternal life with God.

Holy Spirit One person of the threefold nature of God.

Incarnate The doctrine that God took human form in Jesus.

monotheism Belief in one God.

resurrection The rising from the dead of Jesus Christ on the third day after the crucifixion.

Son One person of the threefold nature of God.

Teleological argument The argument that the world is so complex that it must have had a designer and the designer must have been God.

Trinity The Christian belief that God is three separate persons within One – Father, Son and Holy Spirit.

Ontological argument The argument based on the idea that God is greater than anything else people can think of.

GET STARTED

Is there something you believe in although you cannot prove it exists? Try to prepare a justification of this belief.

Mass at St Peter's Basilica in the Vatican City, Italy.

Beliefs about the nature of God

The next two pages will help you to:

- explore what Christians believe about the nature of God
- explain Christian beliefs about the Trinity.

What do Christians believe about God?

Christians believe that there is only one God – this is called **monotheism**. They also believe that God is not like any other living being and this makes it difficult to describe God. One word they do use is holy and this means special, pure and set apart.

Here are some of the qualities that Christians attribute to God.

The Trinity

Christians suggest that God can be understood in three different ways, rather like the way water can take three different forms.

This does not mean that Christians believe there is more than one God, but that there are three different aspects of God.

God the Father: God in Heaven

For Christians, the image of the **Father** suggests that God loves human beings – God is the creator and sustainer of **Heaven** and earth and cares for everyone and everything. God also acts as a judge and will punish humans if they do wrong. However, God will forgive if they show they are sorry. God is Almighty (powerful) – a 'Loving Parent'. It is important to remember that although, traditionally and in this book, God is usually referred to as 'he', many Christians believe that God has no gender and may refer to God as a mother.

Genesis 1:1

In the beginning God created the Heavens and the earth.

God the Son: God in the form of Jesus

Christians believe that Jesus was the **Son** of God, God **incarnate** – fully God and fully human. Jesus was born of a human mother and lived a human life (but was sinless). Jesus showed people how to live in the right way so that they could enter the kingdom of **Heaven**. Jesus showed God's love by being crucified so that humans could be forgiven for their wrongdoing. Christians believe that God showed power over death when Jesus rose from the dead – the **resurrection**. Jesus ascended to Heaven and at the end of time he will come as judge.

AO1 skills ACTIVITIES

Think about the superheroes you have seen on television or film. Make a spider diagram to show their qualities and skills. Add any other things you think a supreme being should be able to do. Compare your results with someone else.

God the Holy Spirit: God at work in the world

After the resurrection, Jesus stayed on earth for a short time and he worked with his disciples (followers). He then went to Heaven – the ascension – and God sent the **Holy Spirit**, the Power of God at work in the world today to guide and support Christians.

Although the **Trinity** can be simplified in symbols such as a trefoil or clover leaf, it is a complex idea which was developed, after much discussion, by Christians during the 4th century CE. The doctrine of the Trinity has been described as one of the most difficult areas for people to understand.

The core beliefs about God are found in the Apostles' Creed.

It is important to remember that Christians are monotheists which means that they believe there is just one God even though the doctrine of the Trinity says that this one God has three forms.

Christians also believe that God has a number of attributes or characteristics:

- Omnipotent: this means that God is all-powerful and can do anything.
- Omniscient: God knows everything.
- Omnipresent: God is everywhere at the same time.
- Omnibenevolent: God is all-good and all-loving.

The Apostles' Creed

I believe in one God, the Father almighty, creator of Heaven and earth.
I believe in Jesus Christ, his only Son, our Lord, who was conceived by the Holy Spirit, born of the Virgin Mary.
Suffered under Pontius Pilate, was crucified, died and was buried; he descended to the dead.
On the third day he rose again, he ascended into Heaven, he is seated at the right hand of the Father, and he will come to judge the living and the dead.
I believe in the Holy Spirit, the holy Catholic Church, the communion of saints, the forgiveness of sins, the resurrection of the body, and the life everlasting.
Amen

AO2 skills ACTIVITIES

'The Trinity is too complicated, Christians should just say that there is one God.' Do you agree? How might a Christian respond to this statement?

Reasons Christians believe in God

The next two pages will help you to:

- examine the reasons Christians give for believing in God
- examine the strengths and weaknesses of these reasons
- evaluate how convincing you find these reasons.

Why do Christians believe in God?

The following are some of the reasons why a **Christian** might believe in God.

Ontological Argument

One Christian thinker, Anselm (1033–1109) said that God should be described as 'that which nothing greater can be conceived'. This means that God must exist otherwise we could not produce this description.

Cosmological Argument

Thomas Aquinas (1225–74) argued that something cannot come from nothing. He carried on to say that, therefore, because there is a universe, someone or something must have brought it into existence. He said that this 'first cause' of the universe was God.

A watch is so complex someone must have designed it.

However, although Aquinas said that this 'first cause' of the universe was God there is no proof of this statement. It is possible that there was a 'first cause' of the universe but that this was not God.

Teleological Argument (design argument)

A Christian philosopher, William Paley (1734–1805), produced a theory which has become known as the Divine Watchmaker. Paley said that if you were walking across a field and saw a large rock you would just assume that it had always been there. However, if you also found a watch in the field you would assume that its parts had not come together by chance but that someone had designed it. He then applied these ideas to the world and God and said that the world was so complicated that it could not have come into existence by chance. If the world did not appear by chance then it must have been designed and that designer must have been God. Einstein (1879–1955) suggested that the design of the world must have had a 'helping hand' and that this hand was God.

This argument has been criticised because people say that the fact that a design is complicated does not prove the existence of a god and also does not prove that it was only one god who was responsible.

AO1 skills **ACTIVITIES**

Make a list of five things which you believe in but cannot prove. For example, you might say that you believe in Father Christmas or the Tooth Fairy though you probably won't. Compare your list with a partner. Explain why you believe in these things.

Argument from experience

Some people have argued that God can be experienced. This may be through incidents such as answers to prayers or the experience of miracles. Because people have experienced these things they argue that therefore God must exist. For some people, a personal experience of God may have convinced them that God exists: for example, New York ex-gang member Nicky Cruz, who experienced a religious conversion.

People have argued against this because often there is very little evidence to show that someone has had a religious experience or that a miracle has actually happened.

Moral Argument

This argument says that people all have a basic understanding of what is 'right' and 'wrong' which is often called the conscience. If this is the case then where did this knowledge or conscience come from? The only answer to this must be from God. Others suggest that the feeling of guilt if we do wrong is God, who knows our actions even if no one else does. However, if everyone's conscience comes from God, why do all people not believe that the same things are right and wrong? Also, why do Christians not always agree on what is right and wrong?

Background and Upbringing

People brought up in a Christian family may accept that God exists because they have always been taught so. They may go to church on Sundays and celebrate festivals and special occasions but they might not be able to say why they believe that God exists only that they believe he does.

Many people would say that this sort of 'blind faith' does not show the existence of God at all and is just the result of upbringing. Others might argue that the reason the family believes and has passed on their faith is because it is true and that this is God at work.

Sometimes people see science and religion as opposing each other. However, it is worth remembering that some famous scientists such as John Polkinghorne are Christians while others like Richard Dawkins are atheists.

Albert Einstein (1879–1955).

RESEARCH NOTE

Go to the Nicky Cruz website to help you write a diary showing how Nicky Cruz felt his life was changed by his religious experience.

ACTIVITIES

'If there was a God we would be able to prove it.' Do you agree? How might a Christian respond to this statement?

Miracles in the Bible

The next two pages will help you to:

- examine miracles in the Old and New Testaments of the Bible
- understand the importance of Biblical miracles for Christians.

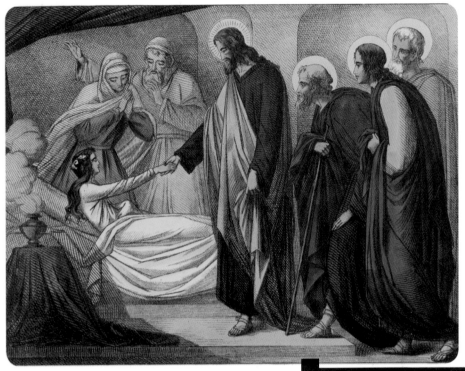

Jesus brings the daughter of Jairus back to life.

AO1 skills ACTIVITIES

Over a week, look at news reports in papers, on the Internet and on television. Collect three examples of modern miraculous events. Make a group collage to show the variety of events in the world that are not easily explained by rational and scientific explanations.

Miracles in Christianity

A miracle is a marvellous event that cannot be explained by any human activity. It is said, by a **Christian**, to be evidence of God intervening in the world at a time of crisis. Christians say this happens because God is omnipotent. In the New Testament, two terms are used to describe miraculous events – 'mighty works' and 'signs'.

Miracles in the Old Testament

There are many examples of miracles in the Old Testament. Many of these show God intervening in the world to help the Israelites. When Moses was leading the Israelites out of Egypt they were pursued by Pharaoh's armies. Moses needed his people to cross the Red Sea.

Exodus 14:21–22

Then Moses stretched out his hand over the sea, and all that night the LORD drove the sea back with a strong east wind and turned it into dry land. The waters were divided, and the Israelites went through the sea on dry ground, with a wall of water on their right and on their left.

Another Old Testament miracle occurs when the Israelites, on their way back to the Promised Land, had to fight the Amorites. This story can be found in Joshua 10. On this occasion God decided to help the Israelites by throwing giant hailstones from **Heaven** which killed many of the Amorites. Also God gave the Israelites more time to fight the battle. In order to do this he stopped the sun moving in the sky and gave the Israelites a full day of sunlight to fight.

These two miracles both show God intervening in the world in a very dramatic and physical way.

Miracles in the New Testament

Christians believe that the most important example of God's intervention in the world was in God taking human form as his **Son**, Jesus, known as the **incarnation**. Also, the miracle stories in the New Testament show the presence and love of God at work in the world through the actions of Jesus.

The miracles of Jesus

There are a number of accounts of miracles performed by Jesus in the four gospels (Matthew, Mark, Luke and John). Miracles in the New Testament can be divided into four main groups, as follows:

- natural miracles: Mark 4:35–41 – Jesus calms a storm at sea
- casting out demons: Mark 7:24–30 – Jesus casts a demon out of a Syrophoenician woman
- healing the sick: Mark 10:46–52 – Jesus restores the sight of a blind man called Bartimaeus
- raising the dead: Mark 5:22–42 – Jesus brings the daughter of Jairus back to life.

Christians would also say that the final miracle and perhaps the greatest one was the **resurrection** of Jesus and the appearances he made to his followers after his death.

The first miracle Jesus performed was a natural miracle, at a wedding in Cana.

John 2:1–3, 6–9a

On the third day, a wedding took place at Cana in Galilee. Jesus' mother was there, and Jesus and his disciples had also been invited to the wedding. When the wine was gone, Jesus' mother said to him, 'They have no more wine.'
Nearby stood six stone water jars, the kind used by the Jews for ceremonial washing, each holding from twenty to thirty gallons. Jesus said to the servants, 'Fill the jars with water,' so they filled them to the brim. Then he told them, 'Now draw some out and take it to the master of the banquet.'
They did so, and the master of the banquet tasted the water that had been turned into wine. He did not realise where it had come from, though the servants who had drawn the water knew.

A miracle also occurred when the **Holy Spirit** descended on the disciples who were together on the day of Pentecost. They heard a violent wind from Heaven which filled the house and then tongues of fire rested on each of them. The disciples were filled with the power of the Holy Spirit and found that they were able to speak in different languages. (You can read the whole account of this in Acts 2.)

MUST THINK ABOUT!

Miracles mean that the laws which govern the universe have been broken.

ACTIVITIES

'If God made the rules of science and the world he would not break them by performing miracles.' Do you agree? How might a Christian respond to this statement?

Miracles today

The next two pages will help you to:

- examine miracles in recent centuries
- explore the importance of these miracles for Christians.

The grotto at Lourdes, France.

Modern miracles

A **Christian** may ask God for a miracle to help them in a crisis: for example, when a loved one is suffering an illness. They may also thank God when a miraculous event has occurred. Throughout the history of Christianity there have been many thousands of incidents which have been claimed as miracles. The details of many of these are now, of course, lost. Over the past two hundred years there have been several occasions of miraculous events.

Lourdes, France

Marie-Bernard Soubirous (Saint Bernadette 1844–79) was a poor shepherdess. On 11 February 1858 she was searching for wood with her sister and a friend. She looked across at the left bank of the stream and saw an apparition – a vision of a beautiful lady standing in the Massabielle grotto. Bernadette called her 'a small young lady' or 'that thing' but the townspeople, hearing of the visions, soon decided that this was the Virgin Mary. There were 18 visions which ended on 16 July.

During the third vision which took place on 18 February the Virgin spoke for the first time. She told Bernadette that she did not need to write down what she would say and asked her, 'Would you do me the kindness of coming here for 15 days?' and then said, 'I do not promise to make you happy in this world but in the other.'

AO1 skills **ACTIVITIES**

What would be a real miracle? Make a list with a partner and discuss why you have both included what you have.

MUST THINK ABOUT!

Although many people have recovered from illnesses after visiting Lourdes, the Roman Catholic Church investigates each claim very carefully and since the first 'official' cure on 1 March 1858, only 66 cases have been accepted as genuinely miraculous by the Church.

At the ninth vision Bernadette was told to 'drink from the fountain' and although she could see no water, she did as she was told and dug in the earth until a bubbling pool of water appeared. During the thirteenth Apparition the Virgin said 'Go, tell the priests to come here in procession and build a chapel here.'

On 25 March 1858, during the sixteenth Apparition, Bernadette went to the Grotto and asked the Lady for her name. She asked three times until, finally, she received the answer 'Que soy era Immaculada Conceptiou' (I am the Immaculate Conception). In 1862 Pope Pius IX approved the visions as authentic and authorised a prayer to Mary as Our Lady of Lourdes.

In 1866 Bernadette joined the Sisters of Charity and in 1877 she became a nun. She was recognised as a Saint by the Church in 1933. The underground spring in the grotto is believed to have healing powers and more than five million pilgrims visit Lourdes every year in the hope of a cure, either for themselves or others.

Knock, Ireland

On 21 August 1879, Mary McLoughlin, the housekeeper of the parish priest of Knock, County Mayo, Ireland saw an image of the Virgin Mary, St Joseph and St John on the south wall of the church.

It was night time and the wall was bathed in a mysterious light. She ran to the home of a friend, Margaret Byrne whose sister, Mary, offered to walk back with her. As they approached the church they both saw the figures. The figure of the Blessed Virgin was life-size, while the other two seemed smaller. They were about two feet from the ground. Mary was looking up to **Heaven** and wore a large white cloak and a crown.

More than a dozen people saw the vision which lasted for about three hours before fading away. One witness reported that 'The figures were fully rounded, as if they had a body and life. They did not speak but, as we drew near, they retreated a little towards the wall.' The church authorities were sceptical but pilgrimages to the church at Knock began in 1880 and two years later Archbishop John Joseph Lynch of Toronto visited Knock and claimed he had been healed by the Virgin of Knock.

Knock has become a centre for over half a million people a year making pilgrimages to honour the vision or to ask for healing. The church of Our Lady Queen of Ireland holds over 2000 worshippers.

The shrine in Knock, Ireland.

AO2 skills ACTIVITIES

'People should not believe in miracles unless they see them for themselves.' Do you agree? How might a Christian respond to this statement?

Remember and Reflect

The questions in this section are based on the work you have done throughout this Topic. Try to complete as many questions as you can.

The questions in set 1 are designed to test your factual recall and AO1 level skills (knowledge and understanding). The page numbers alongside the questions will help you to find information that might be useful for your answers. Use them to check against what you have written.

The questions in set 2 are more challenging, using AO2 level skills (use of evidence and reasoned argument to evaluate personal responses and differing viewpoints). Your answers many come from more than one part of the Topic.

AO1 Describe, explain and analyse, using knowledge and understanding

Find the answer on:

Question	Find the answer on:
1 What is meant by omnipotent, omniscient and omnipresent?	PAGE 5
2 Name the three persons of the Trinity.	PAGE 4, 5
3 Where could you find teachings about the Trinity?	PAGE 4, 5
4 What is meant by 'incarnate'?	PAGE 4
5 Explain the Cosmological argument.	PAGE 6
6 Explain the Ontological argument.	PAGE 6
7 Explain the Teleological argument.	PAGE 6
8 Explain what is meant by a miracle.	PAGE 8
9 Why did God part the Red Sea?	PAGE 8
10 Give an example of a New Testament miracle.	PAGE 9
11 Where is Lourdes?	PAGE 10
12 Who was Mary McLoughlin?	PAGE 11
13 Which Archbishop was healed at Knock?	PAGE 11
14 Which Pope visited Knock in 1979?	PAGE 11

AO2 Use evidence and reasoned argument to express and evaluate personal responses, informed insights, and differing viewpoints

1 'There is no way of knowing what God is like.' Do you agree with this statement? Explain your thinking on this issue.

2 'Believing in God is no longer important.' Construct a set of arguments for and against this statement.

3 What do you think a Christian would say to the following question: 'Why does God not perform miracles today?'

4 'The story of Paley's watch proves that God exists.' Do you agree with this statement? Explain your thinking on this issue.

5 'People in the 21st century cannot be expected to believe in a Virgin birth.' Do you agree with this statement? Explain your thinking on this issue.

6 'Just because we can tell right from wrong does not mean that God exists.' Construct a paragraph that a Christian might write in response to this statement.

7 'If they are ill people should go to a doctor not a shrine.' Consider the arguments for and against this statement and weigh these up to come to a conclusion.

8 Copy and complete the table below to show how a Christian, a non-believer, and you would respond to the statements. (Remember: not all religious believers agree on everything, so try to reflect this in your answers.) Make sure you include reference to religious knowledge and give as many reasons for each view as possible.

Statement	What would a Christian say and why?	What would a non-believer say and why?	What would you say and why?
Miracles happen			
The Trinity means that Christians believe in three gods			
God cannot be good because he lets people suffer			
People only believe in God because their family tells them to			

GradeStudio

Welcome to the Grade Studio

Grade Studio is here to help you improve your answers by working through typical questions you might find on an examination paper. You will see different answers to the questions, showing you how you can improve each answer to get a better grade. There is not sufficient space in this book to give full answers so these answers offer you the skeleton structure of a response. In the exam you must answer as fully as you can.

How the grades work

OCR questions in Spec B always consist of five parts, **a–e**. Parts **a–c** test factual recall only (AO1). Part **d** is always a six-mark question testing understanding (AO1), and part **e** is always a 12-mark question testing evaluation and other AO2 skills.

For parts **a–c**, you need to revise the material for the Topic and make sure that you know it thoroughly – Grade Studio cannot help you with this!

However, for parts **d** and **e** you need to structure your answers to show your skills – and this is where you can use the Grade Studio to help you improve your answers.

Examiners use levels to measure the responses (these are marked in the answers below). You can find the actual levels that examiners will use to mark your answers on pages x–xi.

Graded examples for this topic

AO1

Assessment Objective one (AO1) requires you to 'describe, explain and analyse, using knowledge and understanding'. Here is an example of an AO1 question, along with a student's answers and an examiner's comments on those answers.

Question

Explain why Christians believe in God.   **[6 marks]**

Student's answer

Christians believe in God because this is the teaching they find in the Bible, which is the main source of belief and teachings for Christians.
Some Christians might also believe in God because they believe that miracles happened in the past in the Bible and continue to happen in the present. This includes miracles at places like Lourdes, where sick people go to be healed. Some Christians say that they believe in God because they have prayed to God and their prayers have been answered.

Comments

The candidate has given a satisfactory answer to the question. There are several relevant points but only one of them, the miracles at Lourdes, is explained in any detail. The answer needs to give more information and examples in order to reach Level 3. The candidate could also use more technical terms from the specification to show the breadth of their knowledge and understanding.

Assessment Objective two (AO2) requires you to 'use evidence and reasoned argument to express and evaluate personal responses, informed insights, and differing viewpoints'. Here is an example of an AO2 question, along with a student's answers and an examiner's comments on those answers.

Question

If God existed, we would know it.' Discuss this statement. You should include different, supported points of view and a personal viewpoint. You must refer to Christianity in your answer. **[12 marks]**

Student's answer

Christians might say that they do know that God exists because they can see God's work all around them in the world. Some Christians might also say that they know God exists because God sometimes answers their prayers and they know people who have been made better after people have prayed for them.

Comments

The candidate has given a limited answer to the question. There are two relevant points but they both address the same point of view and neither is expanded very far. The answer needs to give alternative viewpoints, and to include a personal response to reach Level 4.

Student's improved answer

Christians might say that they do know that God exists because they can see God's work all around them in the world. Some Christians might also say that they know God exists because God sometimes answers their prayers and they know people who have been made better after people have prayed for them.

Some people, on the other hand, might think that because of the amount of suffering, disease and poverty in the world, there cannot be a God and if there is one then God is not a good God.

My personal opinion is that there is not enough evidence either way to decide whether God exists or not. There are some events, such as miracles, that suggest that God does exist while other things like the Boxing Day Tsunami seem to suggest that there is no God. So God may exist, but I do not believe that we can 'know' this – it is a matter of faith.

Comments

This is now a good answer to the question although it needs to be expanded to improve even further. The candidate has shown a clear understanding of the question and has presented a range of views supported by evidence and argument. The answer refers to Christian views, among others, and includes a personal viewpoint, which is also supported.

These specimen answers provide an outline of how you could construct your response. Space does not allow us to give a full response. You will need to provide more detail in your actual exam responses.

Topic 2: Religious and spiritual experience

The Big Picture

In this Topic, you will be addressing Christian beliefs and teachings about:

- public and private worship
- prayer and meditation
- food and fasting.

You will also think about your own feelings and responses to these questions and issues.

DID YOU KNOW?

- Christianity is the largest world religion with over 2 billion followers worldwide.

- The Lord's Prayer is probably the best-known Christian prayer and unites Christian denominations across the world.

- Many Christians believe they have spiritual experiences through prayer and worship. They connect and communicate directly with God.

KEY WORDS

crucifix Cross with the representation of Jesus on it, often a symbol of Christianity found in holy buildings or worn by many Christians on a necklace.

denomination A branch of Christianity.

Eucharist The Christian ceremony commemorating the Last Supper, in which bread and wine are consecrated and consumed. Also known as the Mass or Holy Communion.

fasting To go without food or something else chosen by an individual; in religion it is to empathise with others and try to get closer to God.

icons Images or pictures which are used to aid focus and concentration in prayer.

Lord's Prayer Probably the most well-known prayer in Christianity, taught by Jesus to his followers.

meditation An idea connected to prayer and worship where an individual is occupied in thought and reflects deeply on spiritual matters or may concentrate on an idea or object.

prayer Communication with God, either individually and privately or communally with others.

ritual Order and set approach to worship, where the same actions may be performed.

sermon A talk given by a minister which highlights an important issue or topic.

symbol A picture or image that represents something else, it usually has a deeper or more significant meaning.

Trinity The Christian belief that God is three separate persons within One – Father, Son and Holy Spirit.

worship A way of honouring or respecting God with great devotion.

What is a spiritual experience?

 **GET STARTED**

Think of a hobby or activity that you enjoy. Make a list of ways in which you show dedication and commitment to this. What similarities may there be with a religious believer showing commitment to their faith?

Public and private worship (1)

The next two pages will help you to:

- explore the concept of Christian worship
- examine the key features of public and private worship
- reflect on the part played by respect and devotion in your own experiences.

Concept of worship

Worship is seen by Christians to be an act of respect or devotion to God. It is paying special attention to God and showing he is important. It is a way of honouring God and developing a relationship with him. Different denominations within the Christian Church emphasise different forms and follow different patterns of worship. Christians worship God to show their love and commitment to him, to thank or praise him, to ask for help or guidance, to ask for forgiveness or strengthen their faith and become closer to God.

Christians worship privately at home and communally in specially designed buildings. Worship is often seen as devotion and commitment to God. There are many key features of worship including **prayer**, singing, **meditation**, readings from the Bible and a talk or **sermon** from a priest or vicar.

Prayer is an essential part of Christian worship.

What are the key features of public worship?

The majority of Christians worship in a holy building. The Church is the most common religious building but they also have Cathedrals; large, ornate places of worship and Chapels; localised small community places of worship. Different names can be used for the buildings, for example Quakers (the Religious Society of Friends) worship in a Meeting House. Whatever the name used, they are all designed to assist Christian believers in their worship of God and include many elements that show devotion and respect to him.

The Christian holy building provides a place for believers who hold similar ideas to come together and share in their faith and worship of God. The most common form of worship is the **Eucharist** (meaning 'giving thanks'). It is also known as the service of Holy Communion, Mass or the Lord's Supper. It is a service where bread and wine are shared in commemoration of the Last Supper Jesus shared with his disciples before his death. It is an opportunity for Christians to be united in their beliefs and show respect and devotion to God.

 **ACTIVITIES**

Make a list of reasons why it is important to show respect to others. Make a second list showing ways in which Christians show respect to God.

> **Matthew 26: 26–28**
>
> *Jesus took the bread, gave thanks and broke it, and gave it to his disciples, saying 'Take and eat; this is my body.' Then he took the cup, gave thanks, and offered it to them, saying, 'Drink from it, all of you. This is my blood of the new covenant, which is poured out for many for the forgiveness of sins.'*

The ceremony of public worship

Public worship takes on a variety of forms. Many Churches have a service book that contains the pattern for their worship. Hymns are sung which reflect Christian beliefs about God and the Christian faith. They are often prayers set to music. Readings from the Bible are given which provide teachings from Christianity and a sermon (talk by the priest or vicar) is given.

Communal prayers also take place in services, allowing a group of Christians to communicate with God. Formal worship, based upon a set pattern is often elaborate, colourful and full of ritual. Many Christians will individually make signs to demonstrate their respect to God in a holy building such as bowing before the altar or making the sign of the cross over their bodies. This symbolises not only the devotion of the believer, but also the state of mind that the worshipper is adopting.

Some Christian denominations, such as Evangelical churches, promote interactive services where singing and dancing feature prominently. Others adopt less formal and set patterns to their worship, emphasising silent worship or only speaking when they want to express themselves. The common element of public worship is showing respect and devotion to God.

Through coming together in a place of worship, Christians are encouraged to demonstrate their commitment to God and they can take strength from sharing together in their faith. Going to a religious building is important to a Christian and occupies a significant place in their lives.

What are the key features of private worship?

Some Christians also adopt elements of private worship. They do not simply worship God in Church but also regularly throughout their daily lives. Some Christians put aside time to reflect on their beliefs or read passages from the Bible. They may join Bible study groups to discuss their faith and religious teachings. Prayer is an important feature of private worship and believers can communicate directly with God.

Regular prayers and personal devotions bring Christians closer to God and develop a personal relationship with him. Individual prayers offer an opportunity for Christians to communicate with God about personal issues not appropriate during public services. Private worship could also take the form of helping others. Serving and helping others is a way of experiencing God, putting his teachings into practice.

MUST THINK ABOUT!

What are the advantages and disadvantages of having so much variety in Christian worship?

Our Father...

AO2 skills ACTIVITIES

Think about someone you respect and admire. It may be someone famous or someone close to you. Why do they inspire you and why do you look up to them? What similarities may there be with a Christian looking up to and respecting God?

Public and private worship (2)

How is symbolism used in worship?

Symbolism has always featured prominently within Christianity. A **symbol** is an image or picture that represents something else, usually having a deeper or more significant meaning. Symbolism features prominently within Christianity and is a major feature within **worship**.

Physical symbols can be found in holy buildings and many elements of worship are symbolic. They are used to help believers focus on their faith and worship God. However, symbolism within Christianity is used on different levels; some Christian buildings are full of symbols whilst others feel symbols can be distracting and lessen concentration, preferring to worship in plain surroundings.

The most prominent Christian symbols are the cross and **crucifix**. Both are found in places of worship or worn as symbols by believers. The crucifix reminds Christians of the sacrifice Jesus made through his death whilst the empty cross symbolises the celebration of Jesus defeating sin by rising from the dead. Many Churches are built in the shape of a cross. Many are also built facing east, the direction of the rising sun, marking the beginning of a new day and source of light, symbolising the Christian belief in Jesus' resurrection.

The Chi-Rho is another common symbol, made of the first two letters of the Greek word Christ. The Alpha and Omega are taken from the Greek alphabet using the first and last letters reminding Christians that God was the first in the world (as creator) and will be the last in the world (as judge).

The fish symbol – ICTHUS – was originally a secret symbol used by early Christians who were afraid of Roman persecution. The letters symbolise the Christian belief in 'Jesus Christ God's Son Saviour'. The three points also remind Christians of the **Trinity**, the belief that God is One but understood through three distinct parts – Father, Son and Holy Spirit.

The next two pages will help you to:

- examine how symbolism is used in worship
- evaluate the importance of symbolism in worship
- explore the use of art and music in Christian worship.

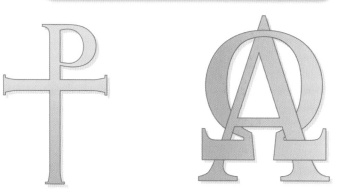

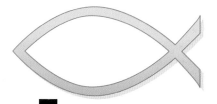

Some examples of Christian symbols are the Chi-Rho, Alpha and Omega, Icthus.

AO1 skills **ACTIVITIES**

Design a stained glass window using some of the symbols suggested and any other Christian symbols you know.

Various other symbols are used in Christian worship. The dove is used to represent peace. Icons and images of Mary, Jesus and various Saints are also found in holy buildings and used as aids to worship.

How important is the use of symbolism in worship?

Symbols are a main feature of Christianity and this shows the importance attributed to them. They have a long history within the faith and are a significant way of expressing or identifying a person who follows Christianity. It is clear that they are given prominence for many different reasons.

Symbols are important within Christian worship because:

- they help convey a deeper meaning or understanding for Christians
- they remind Christians about aspects of their faith
- they help Christians focus on God when they are praying or worshipping
- they are visual reminders of their beliefs
- they help identify Christians and demonstrate their faith to others
- they help Christians feel closer to God and worship him in a personal way.

How can art and music be used to express beliefs about God?

Art and music are forms of expression that help to express complex ideas. They are used by many Christians as expressions of faith and help to convey challenging ideas.

Many famous paintings are associated with religious ideas. Judgement, Jesus and the Trinity are three examples. Some Churches may have examples of religious art hung on the wall. However, some Christians may prefer not to have images when they are worshipping as it distracts their focus from God. They are careful to point out that communication is worship between the individual and God and a form of focus is not always necessary.

Music features prominently in Christian worship. It unites believers and provides a form of expression. It may be compared to the sense of union gained from joining together to sing or chant and support a football team. Christian music can be diverse. Prayers can be sung and in some traditions, it is common for entire services to be chanted. Hymns feature in many worship services and an organ may be used to accompany singing. Evangelical Churches, in particular, may include spontaneous music while many others such as Gospel Churches use music to express their joy for their faith.

MUST THINK ABOUT!

Symbols help to portray hidden or deeper meanings. If you were asked to create a symbol to reveal something about you, what would you draw and why?

RESEARCH NOTE

Research three examples of popular hymns sung during Church services and three examples of famous pieces of religious art. Study them carefully and note down what religious ideas they contain.

 **ACTIVITIES**

Why do you think music and art are effective methods of conveying difficult ideas? What modern ideas might be conveyed in this way?

Prayer and meditation

The next two pages will help you to:

- explore the concept of Christian prayer and its purpose in worship
- explore the importance of prayer and how it can help to deepen faith.

What is prayer?

Prayer is a form of communication with God. Just as you may talk to people in order to develop a relationship with them, Christians feel it is important to talk to God in order to develop a relationship with him. Prayers can be said publicly or privately and may be spoken or silent. Christians feel they are closest to God when praying. **Meditation** is a quiet form of prayer where the worshipper seeks to concentrate their mind on God or spiritual matters. Set prayers may be part of a formal service allowing worshippers to communally speak to God.

Private **worship** offers more opportunity for personal responses. Christians may spend time alone in silent reflection or contemplation, which provides the chance to develop a close and personal relationship with God.

Perhaps the most well-known Christian prayer is the Lord's Prayer. In the Bible, Jesus taught his followers how to pray. The Lord's Prayer includes the themes of confession, thankfulness for what God has provided, adoration of him, concern for others and being humble. This prayer is used in Church services as well as being a source of private worship.

AO1 skills ACTIVITIES

Read through the Lord's Prayer and then try to write a modern version of it in your own words.

> *Our Father, who art in heaven, hallowed be thy name.*
> **This shows respect to God and recognises he is holy**
> *Thy kingdom come, thy will be done; on earth as it is in heaven.*
> **Asks for God's help in the world**
> *Give us this day our daily bread*
> **Asks for God to provide**
> *And forgive us our trespasses, as we forgive those who trespass against us,*
> **Requests forgiveness for wrongdoings and recognises people must forgive others**
> *And lead us not into temptation, but deliver us from evil.*
> **Asks for God's protection**
> *For thine is the kingdom, the power, and the glory for ever and ever. Amen.*
> **Ends with praise and thanks as well as recognition of God's power.**

Many Christians feel that a set prayer helps them to concentrate on God and communicate with him. They can think about the words they are saying and shut out everyday life in order to show respect and devotion to God. Some Christians however, feel that there is room for spontaneity within worship and prayers. They may want to move away from using formal set prayers and say their own, which may be more appropriate to the moment or reason for prayer.

What is the purpose of prayer?

There are many reasons why people pray including:

- to ask for help, strength or guidance
- to give thanks for someone
- to confess sins
- to feel closer to God and develop a relationship with him
- to meditate in worship
- to follow the example set by Jesus
- to bring comfort in times of need.

How can prayer help to deepen faith?

Prayer is a method of communication and can bring Christians closer to God. As they develop a relationship with him, they are more aware of their beliefs, therefore deepening their faith further. Meditation plays an important role allowing reflection and time to consider spiritual matters. Many aids to worship are used by Christians to help concentration.

Some Christians, especially Roman Catholics, use a rosary, a string of beads with a **crucifix** that helps to focus on the prayers. The repetition of touching the beads allows believers to shut out everything else and this develops a deeper connection between the individual and God. Icons and images can also perform the same function. Prayer can have a major impact upon the life of an individual. It can give hope and meaning to faith.

What is the significance of prayer and prayers being answered?

Prayer is a powerful tool. It is a direct form of communication with God and allows the worshipper to connect with the metaphysical world. Prayer, and indeed Christianity, is about faith. Evidence is not required about God's existence or assertion that Christianity is right; it is more about a connection and trust that the beliefs are correct. Prayer therefore holds a vital role in the practice of demonstrating belief. Prayers being answered also strengthen faith and can also lead to conversion to faith of a previous unbeliever. This demonstrates the power that prayer has in providing comfort to those who need it, direction for those who need guidance and answers for those who seem lost.

FOR DEBATE

Think about the following statement. 'Prayer is no use in the real world as we don't know if God hears them.' Make a list of reasons for and against it before writing your own opinion. Have a class debate to see what others think.

AO2 skills ACTIVITIES

'Praying with others provides more comfort and hope than praying alone.' Discuss this statement. You should include different, supported points of view and a personal viewpoint. You must refer to Christianity in your answer.

Food and fasting

The next two pages will help you to:

- understand the concept of fasting
- explain what special food Christians have
- evaluate your own views on Christian attitudes to food.

For most Christians the Eucharist is the central act of worshipping in church.

What is fasting?

Fasting is when you go without food or drink for a set amount of time. Often the reason for fasting is connected to ideas of purification. In Christianity, many believers feel fasting helps them to concentrate on their faith and allows them to see what life is like for others and sympathise with them. It makes them less selfish and provides opportunity to reflect on others rather than themselves.

How do Christians respond to God by fasting?

The most common time for fasting in Christianity is during Lent. This takes place 40 days before Easter and many Christians choose to give up something they enjoy during this time as part of their **worship** to God. They may give up a particular food to sympathise with the experience of Jesus in the wilderness during the time he was tempted by the devil.

Christians believe that choosing to go without something during this time helps them to remember that they are dependent upon God and he provides for their needs and gives them strength. It is also a reminder of the suffering of Jesus and shows dedication and commitment to their faith. Christians consider this to be an essential element in their development as religious believers.

Many Christians also believe that fasting during Lent is associated with discipline and it teaches them to control their desires and wants. They believe that God is the only one who should be worshipped and nothing else should control them. Many Christians may also choose to fast at times other than Lent to remind themselves not to be greedy and be aware of the experiences and, often, suffering of others. Christians believe that fasting brings them closer to God, allows them to appreciate what God has provided and sympathise with others.

What special food is there for Christian festivals?

There are no set religious laws in Christianity about food. The Bible provides no direct guidance about what Christians should and shouldn't eat. Christians believe that God gave humans plants, animals and fish to eat (Genesis 9:3). Many will refer to the vision of Peter (Acts 10:9–16) that suggests God wants them to eat all kinds of food.

> ### Acts 10:11–15
> *He saw heaven opened and something like a large sheet being let down to earth by its four corners. It contained all kinds of four-footed animals, as well as reptiles of the earth and birds of the air. Then a voice told him, 'Get up, Peter. Kill and eat.' 'Surely not, Lord!' Peter replied. 'I have never eaten anything impure or unclean.' The voice spoke to him a second time, 'Do not call anything impure that God has made clean.'*

Some Christians are vegetarian, however, as they feel they have a responsibility of stewardship to look after the animals in the world. The majority of Christians do not abstain from eating any food for religious reasons but some may be more aware about the conditions in which the food they eat have been kept and may avoid eating animals that have not been cared for humanely. They may be involved in organisations such as Fairtrade which campaigns for producers to be paid fairly.

The **Eucharist** service is the most well-known connection to food. In the service, the bread is used to represent the body of Jesus and the wine, his blood. These remind Christians that Jesus is with them and the bread and wine are consecrated before being received.

Festivals in Christianity are a time for believers to join together and be united in their faith. Food is often used to celebrate these occasions, such as hot cross buns being eaten on Good Friday. The cross reminds Christians of the sacrifice of Jesus. Shrove Tuesday is when pancakes are eaten. These were originally made in preparation for Lent when something is given up. Pancakes used up any leftovers and were symbolic of the preparation involved for Lent and Easter. Special food is also eaten at festivals such as Christmas, although perhaps these are more significant religiously for bringing people together to celebrate the birth of Jesus, as there is no set Biblical guidance of food for Christian festivals.

REMEMBER THIS

Lent is the festival that occurs 40 days before Easter. It is a time of preparation and discipline for Christians.

RESEARCH NOTE

Read the text from Acts 10. Find out why Peter would have said that he had never eaten anything impure or unclean.

ACTIVITIES

'There are no advantages to fasting.' Discuss this statement. You should include different, supported points of view and a personal viewpoint. You must refer to Christianity in your answer.

The questions in this section are based on the work you have done throughout this Topic. Try to complete as many questions as you can.

The questions in set 1 are designed to test your factual recall and AO1 level skills (knowledge and understanding). The page numbers alongside the questions will help you to find information that might be useful for your answers. Use them to check against what you have written.

The questions in set 2 are more challenging, using AO2 level skills (use of evidence and reasoned argument to evaluate personal responses and differing viewpoints). Your answers many come from more than one part of the Topic.

AO1 Describe, explain and analyse, using knowledge and understanding

Find the answer on:

1 Explain what each of the following terms means. Write one sentence for each word: — **PAGE 17**
  a *Eucharist*
  b *fasting*
  c *prayer*
  d *worship*
  e *symbol*

2 Give three reasons why Christians worship God. — **PAGE 18**

3 Give two other names for the Eucharist. — **PAGE 18**

4 Why is the Eucharist important as a form of worship? — **PAGE 18**

5 Explain the difference between public and private worship. — **PAGE 18, 19**

6 Explain three things that may happen during public worship. — **PAGE 19**

7 Describe and explain how a Christian holy building is suited to worship and reflects Christian symbolism. — **PAGE 20**

8 Draw and explain the meaning of three Christian symbols. — **PAGE 21**

9 Give three reasons why symbols are important in Christian worship. — **PAGE 21**

10 Why are art and music good methods of expressing faith? — **PAGE 21**

11 Why is prayer important to Christians? — **PAGE 22, 23**

12 Give two purposes of prayer. — **PAGE 22**

13 Explain two ways in which prayer can deepen the faith of a Christian. — **PAGE 23**

14 Give two reasons why Christians fast. — **PAGE 24**

15 Which part of the Christian year is usually associated with fasting and why? — **PAGE 24, 25**

16 Explain how Christians are responding to God by fasting. — **PAGE 24**

17 Explain what the Bible says about food laws. — **PAGE 25**

AO2 Use evidence and reasoned argument to express and evaluate personal responses, informed insights, and differing viewpoints

1 Answer the following questions giving as much detail as possible:
   a *Do you think public or private worship is more effective? Explain your answer.*
   b *Do you think that symbolism in religion is successful at portraying complex ideas? Try to use examples to support your view.*
   c *Do you agree that prayer has a purpose? Try to give reasons for your opinion.*
   d *Do you think that fasting is a good form of self-discipline? Give evidence for your view.*

2 'People don't need symbols to worship God.' Discuss this statement. You should include different, supported points of view and a personal viewpoint. You must refer to Christianity in your answer.

3 Make a quiz on this topic that includes 20 questions. Write an answer sheet and then get a partner to try to answer your questions.

4 Use the given structure below to produce a speech explaining your opinion on the following statement: 'Public worship is more effective as you have support and comfort from others who believe the same things you do.'

   • I agree/disagree with the statement because...

   • I understand why someone's opinion may differ from mine because...

   • I think a Christian would argue...

   • In conclusion, I feel...

GradeStudio

Welcome to the Grade Studio

Grade Studio is here to help you improve your answers by working through typical questions you might find on an examination paper. For a full explanation of how this feature works and how exam questions are structured, see page 14. For a full explanation of Assessment Objectives and Levels of Response, see pages x–xi in the Introduction.

AO1 Question

Why do some Christians fast?

[6 marks]

Student's answer

Some Christians fast because they believe that this will help them understand how people feel who do not have enough to eat. Other Christians might choose to give up something special during Lent, such as chocolate. They do this to remember the time when Jesus was in the wilderness when he did without food and was alone.

Comments

The candidate has given a satisfactory answer to the question. There are two relevant points but they are not explained in any detail. The answer needs to give more information and examples in order to reach Level 3. The candidate could also use more technical terms from the specification to show the breadth of their knowledge and understanding.

Student's improved answer

Some Christians fast because they believe that this will help them understand how people feel who do not have enough to eat. Other Christians might choose to give up something special during Lent, such as chocolate. They do this to remember the time when Jesus was in the wilderness when he did without food and was alone.

This also serves as a preparation for Lent. Lent leads up to Easter and is a period of penitence (being sorry for what you have done). The forty days of Lent remember the forty days when Jesus fasted and was tempted by the devil in the wilderness.

In the past, many Roman Catholics fasted for 12 hours before they received communion at the Mass, but now they only have to wait for an hour. Many Christians fast on certain days of the year and save the money that they would have spent on food to give to charities that support people in other countries who do not have enough to eat. So, as well as helping others, they are also practising self-discipline.

Comments

This is now a good answer to the question. The candidate has shown a clear understanding of the question. There is good description and explanation of a variety of different reasons why Christians might fast. The candidate has shown some analysis in dealing with the question of fasting. The information is presented clearly and there is good use of technical terms.

AO2 Question

'Everyone should thank God for their food.' Discuss this statement. You should include different, supported points of view and a personal viewpoint. You must refer to Christianity in your answer. **[12 marks]**

Student's answer

Christians might say that they should always thank God for their food and some people say a prayer after meals. Some Christians have Harvest Festivals when they thank God for food because they believe he is responsible for the crops growing well.

Comments

The candidate has given a limited answer to the question. There are two relevant points but they both address the same point of view and neither is expanded very far. The answer needs to give alternative viewpoints and also include a personal response to reach Level 4.

Student's improved answer

Christians might say that they should always thank God for their food and some people say a prayer after meals. Some Christians have Harvest Festivals when they thank God for food because they believe he is responsible for the crops growing well.

Some people, on the other hand, might think that, although they should thank God for their food by saying Grace after meals, taking part in the Offertory during the Eucharist or attending a Harvest Festival, it still seems unjust that some people are thanking God when they already have more food than they can eat, while others thank God for a small amount of food that is not really enough to live on.

My personal opinion is that if people do believe in God then they should thank God for the food they have. He is in control of the world and gives the sun and the rain to make the crops grow. However, I do think that it is hard for some people to thank God for their food when they do not have enough to eat and it makes God seem unjust. If he truly cared for all people he would make sure everyone had enough to eat. I think some people can be forgiven for not being grateful when they do not have enough through no fault of their own.

Comments

This is now a good answer to the question. The candidate has shown a clear understanding of the question and has presented a range of views supported by evidence and argument. The answer explains Christian views, among others, and includes a personal viewpoint, which is also supported.

These specimen answers provide an outline of how you could construct your response. Space does not allow us to give a full response. You will need to provide more detail in your actual exam responses.

Topic 3: The end of life

The Big Picture

In this Topic, you will be addressing Christian beliefs and teachings about:

- body and soul
- life after death
- funeral rites.

You will also think about your own feelings and responses to these questions and issues.

DID YOU KNOW?

- Many people believe it is the soul that makes each person unique. Some may believe it is connected to a person's personality.

- Most people would like to think that death is not the end so that they may be reunited with loved ones again.

- Christians feel it is important to have a funeral for someone who has died both for the deceased and the family and friends left behind.

KEY WORDS

Committal The actions that take place when a body is buried or cremated.

Day of Judgement The day when God will judge everyone according to their actions and faith on earth.

eulogy The speech or talk given at a funeral about the person who has died.

funeral The ceremony or service that occurs after someone has died.

Heaven A Christian idea of paradise where the soul goes after death if it is free from sin to have eternal life with God.

Hell A place that some Christians believe is a punishment after death for those souls that are not free from sin; it is often referred to as a place of torment or suffering without God.

judge The Christian idea of God acting as a judge to determine whether a person goes to Heaven or Hell after death.

Purgatory In some Christian traditions, a condition or state in which good souls receive spiritual cleansing after death, in preparation for Heaven.

redemption The idea that sins can be forgiven and a person can be redeemed. Jesus is often referred to by Christians as the Redeemer as he died for the sins of the whole world.

salvation Jesus came to earth to save people from their sins and achieved salvation through his sacrifice in death on the cross.

soul Christians believe the soul is a non-physical and immortal part of the body that continues after death and is the connection with God.

Commonwealth War Graves Commission (CWGC) burial ground for the dead of the First World War in Ypres, Belgium.

GET STARTED

Words written in memory of a person who has died are known as an epitaph. Epitaphs are often written on gravestones. In pairs, look at the following epitaphs and discuss which show a belief in the afterlife and which do not:

- 'I was not – I have been – I am not – I do not mind.'
- 'In God's keeping.'
- 'Reunited.'
- 'Always remembered.'

Body and soul

The next two pages will help you to:

- examine Christian belief about the body and the soul
- identify Christian beliefs about the relationship between the body and the soul.

What is the soul?

What is the soul?

Christians believe humans have a mind and a body, but would also argue there is something more to humans, making them unique – a soul. Christians believe that everyone has a soul that is invisible and lives on forever. They often see the soul as the part of a person that makes them unique. What a person believes about the soul is likely to affect their views about death and life after death. A person who believes that they have a soul may believe that death is not the end. On the other hand, someone who does not believe that humans have an eternal soul may think that there is nothing beyond earthly life.

Some common ideas of the soul include:

- the part of a human that is not physical
- the part of humans that lives on after the body has died
- the spiritual aspect of a human that makes each person unique from every other
- the part of a human that allows them to relate to God.

MUST THINK ABOUT!

If the soul is something non-physical, where is it within humans? What evidence do we have that it actually exists?

AO1 skills **ACTIVITIES**

How would you define the soul of a person? What words might you use?

Christians believe that every person has a soul that is separate from the physical body. After the body dies, the immortal soul lives on. It is this belief that makes humans distinct from all other creatures. Christians use the teaching from the Bible that God 'created man in his own image' that sets humans apart from all other creatures and suggests they have a divine spark.

It also states in the Bible that all creatures were formed out of the ground but that Adam was formed from the dust of the ground and God 'breathed into his nostrils the breath of life'. Many Christians take this to mean that humans have a soul; a part of them that lives on even after the body dies and makes each human distinct and unique from all others. Many Christians would suggest that the soul is the spiritual part of humans that is connected to God.

Christians believe in the immortality of the soul for many reasons. These include:

- Jesus conquered death when he was resurrected and ascended into **Heaven**.
- There are references in the gospels to Abraham, Moses and Elijah appearing on the earth with Jesus suggesting they live on in a spiritual realm.
- There seems to be something non-material and immortal about the human mind.

What is the relationship between the body and the soul?

Christians believe that the body houses the soul or spirit. Some think that when the body dies, it is the soul that goes to be reunited with God. However the Apostles' creed states 'I believe… in the resurrection of the body' and some Christians debate whether this is a physical or spiritual body. Many refer to St Paul in arguing that the proof of this is with Jesus as God raised him from the dead. Christians believe that this too will happen for them after death if they believe.

Many Christians believe that the soul and the body are sometimes in conflict. The body wants its desires and pleasures to be fulfilled whilst the soul wants to please God. These are not always in harmony with each other but the advice offered by St Paul was that people should let the spirit guide them, indicating that it is the soul that is more important than the physical body.

Christians do not believe in the idea of reincarnation. They accept that there is only one life on earth and life after death is not a physical world. However, they do believe in a Day of Judgement where there will be a resurrection of the body. Everyone will be made to account for their actions on this day and God will **judge** them on their faith and actions on earth.

FOR DEBATE

Make a list of arguments for and against the following statement. 'There is no such thing as the soul; the body is all there is.' Have a class debate to find out what the consensus of the class views are.

AO2 skills ACTIVITIES

Summarise Christian beliefs about the body and the soul in a creative way. You might like to use words and images. Make sure you include all the important information. Identify beliefs you agree with and those you don't and explain your responses and those of Christians.

Life after death (1)

The next two pages will help you to:

- examine Christian ideas about life after death
- explore what Christians believe about Heaven, Hell, Purgatory, salvation, redemption and the suffering of Christ.

The Last Judgement by Michaelangelo in the Sistine Chapel, Vatican City.

What is the Christian idea about life after death?

Christians believe that death is not the end and that there is life after death. Christians cannot explain fully what life after death will be like. They refer to the teachings in the Bible but believe it is part of their journey to be reunited with God and therefore it is impossible to know exact details.

However, general ideas suggest that after death, they will be reunited with loved ones. Jesus promised there would be a place for all who believed in him. Christians believe that death is not the end and that the immortal **soul** continues on a journey of eternal life in **Heaven**, **Hell** or possibly **Purgatory**.

ACTIVITIES

Create a diagram summarising Christian beliefs about life after death.

What do Christians believe about Heaven, Hell and Purgatory?

Christians believe that those who have followed God's way on earth and not sinned will go to Heaven. This is seen as a place free of suffering where they will spend eternity with God. Sinners who repent can also enter Heaven. The Bible includes many references to Heaven and many Christians believe it is a place where evil and suffering do not exist. As Revelation 21:4 states, 'There will be no more death or mourning or crying or pain.'

Some other Christians, particularly Roman Catholics, also believe in Purgatory, where those souls go of people who have died but are not ready to go to Heaven. In the Middle Ages, it was common for rich people to leave money for prayers to be said after their death to decrease their stay in Purgatory.

Some Christians also believe in Hell, a place full of pain and suffering. It is seen as an eternal place without God. In the Medieval period, many pieces of art depicted a frightening view of Hell; it was shown as a place of torment and suffering, often associated with ideas of fire and steam where pain and torture were common elements. Indeed, the idea of Hell was often used to try and get people to be morally good and follow the teachings of Christianity for fear of ending up in Hell.

However, many Christians believe the Biblical descriptions of Hell to be symbolic in order to try and help people understand a very difficult concept. Some Christians offer a different interpretation of Hell, it being an idea where at the point of death, the body and soul both no longer exist.

What do Christians believe about salvation, redemption and the suffering of Christ?

Jesus was crucified on a cross on Good Friday. It is believed by Christians that three days later he rose again and was resurrected, marked today by the festival of Easter. **Salvation** and **redemption** are Christian terms usually associated with Jesus. He is often attributed the titles of 'Saviour of the World' and 'Redeemer', the former meaning he came to earth to save people from their sins and the latter meaning someone who saves others from sin and damnation.

It is believed by Christians that Jesus sacrificed himself on the cross in order to redeem believers from the original sin of Adam and Eve. Jesus' suffering on the cross allowed those who believe in him and follow him to be forgiven for their sins and enter Heaven. Christians believe that it is through the suffering of Christ that people can be forgiven and also achieve Salvation by following the example of Jesus.

RESEARCH NOTE

Use the Internet to research what is meant by 'limbo'.

FOR DEBATE

'If there was a life after death we would know about it.' Discuss.

RESEARCH NOTE

Look up Revelation Chapter 4 in the Bible. Draw images to represent the ideas contained about what Heaven is like. Then write a description in your own words.

ACTIVITIES

'Life does not finish when we die. Death is not the end but a new beginning.' Prepare a speech explaining your opinion on this statement. Try to make your views more convincing by also offering counter-arguments and showing why you don't agree with them.

Life after death (2)

The next two pages will help you to:

- determine what Christianity believes about the role of God as judge
- evaluate the relationship between God as judge, life on earth and the afterlife.

AO1 skills **ACTIVITIES**

Make a list of qualities or characteristics that you would expect a judge to have. How easy do you think it is to uphold these qualities when you have to make a difficult decision?

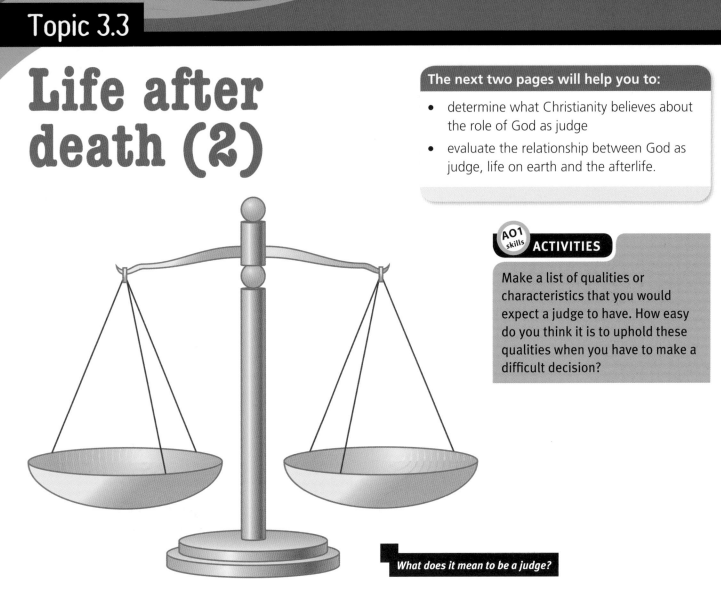

What does it mean to be a judge?

What does Christianity say about God as judge?

Christians attribute two main roles to God. He is eternal and believed to be present at the start of the world as creator and the end of the world as judge. They hold that God is the ultimate and only judge of all humanity. It is after death that Christians believe God will judge each human individually according to the way they have lived their lives, their faith and their actions. Christians believe that God holds all the qualities necessary for a good and fair judge.

According to the Apostles' Creed, God will judge the 'living and the dead' at the end of time. The book of Revelation in the Bible states that there are two books – one containing the deeds people have done in their lives and the other containing the names of all those who have shown belief in the death and resurrection of Jesus. Christians who have believed and responded to Jesus will be rewarded but those who have not will be punished.

How will people be judged?

Christians believe that they will be judged to determine their future in the afterlife on their actions and beliefs on earth. The Bible contains a parable called 'The Sheep and the Goats' that explains how God will judge humans. Parables are stories told by Jesus with a hidden or deeper meaning and were considered a good method of explaining complex ideas to people. The Parable of the Sheep and the Goats is used to teach the idea that when the Day of Judgement comes humans will be separated into two groups. Those who have lived good lives and followed Jesus will be rewarded whilst those who have not are damned to an eternity in **Hell** without God.

What is the relationship between God the judge, life on earth and the afterlife?

There is a very distinct relationship between life on earth, judgement and the afterlife. According to Christians, it is your life and actions on earth that determine how you are judged and where you spend eternity in the afterlife. This has an impact on the behaviour of many Christians as they live their lives always aware of the consequence of the afterlife and will try to lead their lives according to God in order to attain the desired outcome.

As the judgement Christians receive after death depends on their behaviour and faith in God during their life, this encourages many people to live morally, according to the laws of God. Christians believe that they should recognise when they do wrong and confess it to God in order to achieve forgiveness. They must put their trust and faith in God to guide them to eternal life with him in Heaven.

Teachings about judgement and the afterlife are found in the New Testament:

> **Acts 17:31**
> *For he has set a day when he will judge the world with justice by the man he has appointed. He has given proof of this to all men by raising him from the dead.*

> **Romans 2:12, 16**
> *All who sin apart from the law will also perish apart from the law, and all who sin under the law will be judged by the law… this will take place on the day when God will judge men's secrets through Jesus Christ, as my gospel declares.*

RESEARCH NOTE

Read the parable of The Sheep and the Goats in Matthew chapter 25. What kind of actions may determine whether a person goes to Heaven or Hell? How does Jesus respond to this question?

MUST THINK ABOUT!

Would you change anything about your actions or behaviour if you were given evidence that an afterlife really did exist?

RESEARCH NOTE

Find out what is meant by the term 'parousia'.

AO2 skills ACTIVITIES

'Christian beliefs about Heaven and Hell are too old-fashioned for people today.' Do you agree with this statement? Explain your own views and also what a Christian might say.

Funeral rites

The next two pages will help you to:

- examine Christian funeral rites
- evaluate how funeral rites reflect Christian beliefs and their purpose in supporting the bereaved.

ACTIVITIES

Explain what happens during a Christian funeral service.

Funerals should be an occasion of joy as well as sadness as Christians believe that after death they will be with God in heaven.

What are funeral rites?

Funeral rites are the customs and ceremonies that happen after a person has died. Many people will at some point in their life consider their death and how they may like to be remembered. Many people will plan their own funerals if they are given the opportunity so they can be remembered in their own special way. Often people will want to choose suitable words to be spoken or music to be played which held a special meaning for them.

Christians believe that funeral rites are very important. They help those left behind cope with their loss, provide comfort and an opportunity to say goodbye to the deceased. Funerals in Christianity have an important purpose. They often follow a set structure but are flexible enough to be personalised.

What happens at a Christian funeral and how do funeral rites reflect Christian beliefs?

Christian funeral services may vary slightly for each Christian denomination but there are many common elements. Christians can be buried or cremated and often it is left to the wishes of the deceased or if they did not state any preference, their family. Burial used to be preferred but as it is the **soul** which is considered important, many Christians now choose to be cremated.

There are a number of key features in Christian funeral services:

- Bible reading: Often the Bible reading will reflect Christian ideas of the afterlife. John 11:25–26 is a commonly chosen passage which mentions eternal life after death with God.
- Prayers: Prayers are said both for the deceased and also their family and friends left behind. Many prayers focus on asking God to keep the bereaved safe and give them the strength to carry on in their lives. The deceased is entrusted to God's care. Many Roman Catholic services will offer prayers for the deceased in their final journey in the afterlife.
- **Eulogy**: A eulogy is a speech or talk given by the vicar or priest or a close family relative. The life of the deceased is spoken about and remembered with memories being shared.
- Hymns: Hymns are sung during the funeral service. 'The Lord's my Shepherd' is a popular choice. Often they will have been suggested previously by the deceased or chosen by their family.
- Eucharist: Some Christians, particularly Roman Catholics, celebrate the Eucharist during the funeral service. It reminds those present of the death and resurrection of Jesus and brings hope for eternal life after death with God.
- The committal: After the service the body is then buried or cremated – if buried, it is common for more prayers to be said at the graveside. The body is usually committed to the earth with the words, 'Ashes to ashes, dust to dust; in sure and certain hope of the resurrection to eternal life.'

How do funeral rites aim to support the bereaved?

Funeral rites have many aims, both for the deceased and the bereaved. These include:

- It is an acknowledgement that the deceased person is no longer part of this world but is with God.
- The family and friends of the deceased can draw comfort from each other and remember the person they have lost.
- The life of the deceased can be celebrated.
- It is an opportunity for the bereaved to express their feelings and emotions for the deceased and share with others who knew the person in their loss.
- It marks the beginning of life without the deceased and allows the bereaved to gain some sense of closure in knowing they have to move on with their lives.

 **RESEARCH NOTE**

Think about the various parts that occur in a funeral service. How do they reflect Christian teachings about the afterlife?

John 11:25b–26a
I am the resurrection and the life. He who believes in me will live, even though he dies, and whoever lives and believes in me will never die.

AO2 skills **ACTIVITIES**

'Funerals are for the living, not the dead.' Do you agree with this statement? Give reasons to support your answer. Explain how a Christian might respond.

Remember and Reflect

The questions in this section are based on the work you have done throughout this Topic. Try to complete as many questions as you can.

The questions in set 1 are designed to test your factual recall and AO1 level skills (knowledge and understanding). The page numbers alongside the questions will help you to find information that might be useful for your answers. Use them to check against what you have written.

The questions in set 2 are more challenging, using AO2 level skills (use of evidence and reasoned argument to evaluate personal responses and differing viewpoints). Your answers many come from more than one part of the Topic.

AO1 Describe, explain and analyse, using knowledge and understanding

Find the answer on:

1 In your own words, explain what eulogy and funeral mean from a Christian perspective.	PAGE 30
2 Explain, in your own words, the relationship between the body and the soul for Christians.	PAGE 33

3 Describe the Christian views of:
   a Heaven
   b Hell
   c Purgatory
	PAGE 35

4 Explain the terms redemption and salvation in relation to Jesus.	PAGE 35
5 Explain why God is described as a judge.	PAGE 36
6 Explain the parable of 'The Sheep and the Goats' in your own words. What is the meaning of this parable?	PAGE 37
7 Explain how humans will be judged for their place in the afterlife according to Christianity.	PAGE 37
8 Why might a fear of the afterlife cause Christians to try and live a moral life?	PAGE 37
9 Explain four features of a Christian funeral. For each one try to explain how it shows a belief in life after death.	PAGE 39
10 Give two purposes of a funeral.	PAGE 38
11 Describe what happens at a funeral service.	PAGE 39
12 How do funeral rites support the bereaved?	PAGE 39
13 Give three reasons why it is important to have funeral rites.	PAGE 38, 39
14 What are funeral rites?	PAGE 38

AO2 Use evidence and reasoned argument to express and evaluate personal responses, informed insights, and differing viewpoints

1   Answer the following questions giving as much detail as possible in your answers and use evidence to support your views:
    a   *Do you believe humans have a soul? Why or why not?*
    b   *Do you believe in life after death? Why or why not?*
    c   *Do you think funeral rites are important? Why or why not?*
    d   *Does consideration of a possible afterlife make you act or behave in a particular way? Please explain your answer and give examples if appropriate.*

2   'When people die that is the end.' Discuss this statement. You should include different, supported points of view and a personal viewpoint. You must refer to Christianity in your answer.

3   'There is no real evidence that humans have a soul.' Discuss this statement. You should include different, supported points of view and a personal viewpoint. You must refer to Christianity in your answer.

4   Find a film or television programme that contains a funeral service. Watch it carefully and make notes on what they do. How accurate a portrayal is this of a Christian funeral service?

5   Consider the issues below and then write down what a Christian might say as well as your opinion on them:

Issue	What would a Christian say?	My opinion
Heaven and Hell		
Faith and belief in God linked to ideas of the afterlife		
The soul		

GradeStudio

Welcome to the Grade Studio

Grade Studio is here to help you improve your answers by working through typical questions you might find on an examination paper. For a full explanation of how this feature works and how exam questions are structured, see page 14. For a full explanation of Assessment Objectives and Levels of Response, see pages x–xi in the Introduction.

AO1 Question

How might Christian funeral rites reflect beliefs about life after death?   [6 marks]

Student's answer

Christian funerals take place in a church with a priest to show that people believe in Christian ideas about death and another life after death. Christians believe that when they die they will go to one of three places: Heaven, Hell or Purgatory. They think that which one they go to depends on the way you have lived your life. If you have been good, you will go straight to Heaven. If you have been bad, you will go to Hell. If you have been in between, then you will go to Purgatory where you wait until God thinks that you are good enough to go to Heaven.

Comments

The candidate has given a satisfactory answer to the question. There are a number of relevant points but only the distinction between Heaven, Hell and Purgatory is explained. The answer needs to give more information and examples in order to reach Level 3. Also it needs to focus more clearly on the funeral service and how this reflects these beliefs. The candidate could use more technical terms from the specification to show the breadth of their knowledge and understanding.

Student's improved answer

Christian funerals take place in a church with a priest to show that people believe in Christian ideas about death and another life after death. Christians believe that when they die they will go to one of three places: Heaven, Hell or Purgatory. They think that which one they go to depends on the way you have lived your life. If you have been good, you will go straight to Heaven. If you have been bad, you will go to Hell. If you have been in between, then you will go to Purgatory where you wait until God thinks that you are good enough to go to Heaven.

A Christian funeral service reflects these beliefs by emphasising Jesus' promise that Christians will join him in Heaven and continue to live in the hands of God. During the service, the priest or minister talks about how Jesus rose from the dead and reminds the mourners that they will also rise from the dead. The service suggests that death is only a stage in life not the end, as people go on to eternal life with God. This can comfort the mourners who believe that they will eventually see the person again.

Comments

This is now a good answer to the question. The candidate has shown a clear understanding of the question. There is good description and explanation of a variety of different aspects of the funeral service. The candidate has shown some analysis in dealing with the question of resurrection in Heaven. The information is presented clearly and there is good use of technical terms.

AO2 Question

'When people die that is the end.' Discuss this statement. You should include different, supported points of view and a personal viewpoint. You must refer to Christianity in your answer. **[12 marks]**

Student's answer

Christians might say that this statement is not true because they believe that after death people go to Heaven or Hell. Some Christians might also say that Jesus promised that, for his followers, death would not be the end but the beginning of a new life with God in Heaven.

Comments

The candidate has given a limited answer to the question. There are two relevant points but they both address the same point of view and neither is expanded very far. The answer needs to give alternative viewpoints, and include a personal response to reach Level 4.

Student's improved answer

Christians might say that this statement is not true because they believe that after death people go to Heaven or Hell. Some Christians might also say that Jesus promised that, for his followers, death would not be the end but the beginning of a new life with God in Heaven.

Some non-believers, on the other hand, might say that there is absolutely no evidence that there is any form of life after death and that it is just wishful thinking to believe in it. My personal opinion is that there is not enough evidence either way to decide whether there is any life after death or not.

Many people have a very strong faith that there is a life after death and that God will look after them when they die. However, even though the Bible suggests that people go to Heaven, no one has ever come back to say whether this is true or not. Belief in an afterlife just gives comfort to people at a very sad time when they have lost a loved one. Events such as ghosts and near-death experiences can all be explained by science and do not prove anything.

Comments

This is now a good answer to the question. The candidate has shown a clear understanding of the question and has presented a range of views supported by evidence and argument. The answer explains Christian views, among others, and includes a personal viewpoint, which is also supported.

These specimen answers provide an outline of how you could construct your response. Space does not allow us to give a full response. You will need to provide more detail in your actual exam responses.

Topic 4: Good and evil

The Big Picture

In this Topic, you will be addressing Christian beliefs about:

- the concepts of good and evil and the ideas of God and the Devil
- the significance of The Fall and beliefs about Original Sin and redemption
- the problem of evil, the concepts of natural and moral evil and responses to evil
- ways of understanding and coping with suffering
- sources and reasons for behaving morally including the Bible, conscience and faith in Christ.

You will also think about your own feelings and responses to these questions and issues.

DID YOU KNOW?

- Satan is the name given to the angel who rebelled against God in Heaven.
- Many people think that the existence of evil and suffering in the world proves that there is no God.
- The fruit eaten by Adam and Eve in the story of the Fall, Genesis chapter 3, is never actually called an apple, although the lump in a person's neck is known as their 'Adam's apple'.
- The Devil tried to tempt Jesus to worship him.

KEY WORDS

conscience An inner voice or feeling giving guidance on the rightness or wrongness of behaviour.

free will The belief that God created humans with the ability to make moral choices.

Golden rule Jesus' teaching the people that they should treat others as they wish to be treated themselves.

Job Biblical character whose faith is tested.

moral evil Evil and suffering caused by people.

natural evil Evil and suffering caused by natural events such as earthquakes.

omnipotent Powerful, able to do anything.

omniscient All-knowing.

Original Sin The sin which was brought into the world at the Fall and which Christianity teaches everyone is born with.

redemption The idea that sins can be forgiven and a person can be redeemed. Jesus is often referred to by Christians as the Redeemer as he died for the sins of the whole world.

Sacrifice Giving up a life for God.

The Devil/Satan A supernatural evil power.

The Fall The disobedience of Adam and Eve resulting in their expulsion from Eden.

theodicies Arguments justifying why there is evil in the world if God is good.

Phan Thi Kim Phúc (born 1963) is shown here running down the centre of the road after a napalm attack near Trang Bang, South Vietnam. The photograph by Huỳnh Công Ut records the massacre which took place on 8 June 1972.

GET STARTED

'Life is unfair and bad things often happen to good people.'
Compile a class list of ways in which life may seem to be unfair.

Good and evil

The concepts of good and evil

Devastation caused by the Boxing Day Tsunami of 2004.

What is good?

Although we use the word 'good' all the time philosophers have argued for centuries about whether it is possible to define 'goodness'. The philosopher G.E. Moore argued that good is 'indefinable'. Christians believe the teaching of Jesus that God is perfect (Matthew 5:48), that only God is good (Mark 10:18), and that they should try to be like God.

> **Mark 10:17–18**
>
> *As Jesus started on his way a man ran up to him and fell on his knees before him. 'Good teacher,' he asked, 'what must I do to inherit eternal life?' 'Why do you call me good?' Jesus answered. 'No-one is good except God alone.'*

What is evil?

Evil is when bad things such as earthquakes and other natural disasters happen, and when people do bad things such as murder and rape. Evil is sometimes described as separation from God or the absence of good. Christians often refer to 'the problem of evil' because it is difficult for them to accept that a good God could create a world where there is so much evil.

What do Christians believe about God?

Do you think that if God is all-loving and all-powerful he should eliminate evil from the world? This is the big question for Christians. Somehow they have come to terms with the question of how a perfect, all-loving, **omnipotent** and **omniscient** God could allow people to suffer. For hundreds of years philosophers and theologians have tried to present arguments to solve it. These arguments are called **theodicies**.

ACTIVITIES

With a partner make a list of people, living and dead, whom you would describe as 'good'. Make a list of the qualities which you think make these people good. Now do the same for evil. Compare your ideas across the class. How easy or difficult is it to define exactly which qualities make someone good?

Many films such as the Matrix trilogy concern the battle between good and evil.

What do Christians believe about the Devil?

One way Christians have tried to explain evil and suffering is by blaming the **Devil** or **Satan**. Some Christians believe that the Devil exists in a physical form but for most, the Devil is a symbolic way of representing the ultimate evil in opposition to the ultimate good, represented by God.

People have always told stories about the constant battle between good and evil/God and the Devil. You can find examples in the storylines of many popular films, television programmes and books. The Devil is often referred to as Satan and sometimes as Lucifer. There are stories, not included in the Bible, about how Lucifer was the leader of the angels who were driven out of heaven after rebelling against God. The 17th-century poet John Milton developed this story in his famous poem *Paradise Lost*.

There are references to the Devil in the Bible. Jesus was tempted in the wilderness by the Devil who showed him all the worldly power he could have if he worshipped him (Luke 4:4–13). Judas is described in Luke's gospel as being possessed by the Devil when he decided to betray Jesus: 'Then Satan entered Judas, called Iscariot, one of the Twelve. And Judas went to the chief priests and the officers of the temple guard and discussed with them how he might betray Jesus. They were delighted and agreed to give him money' (Luke 22:3–5).

The Fall and Original Sin

The Bible begins with an ancient story about a newly created world where everything was perfect – or was it? This story has major significance for Christian beliefs about good and evil and the origins of sin and suffering.

It tells how God gave Adam and Eve, the first humans, freedom of choice when he created them. However, humans often choose to do wrong. The story teaches that evil came into the world when Adam and Eve made a deliberate decision to disobey God. Christians believe that, because Adam and Eve exercised their **free will** and chose to disobey God, all humans were separated from God. They can only return to God through the sacrifice of Jesus, the son of God, dying on the cross. This is called the **redemption**.

> ### John 3:16
> *For God so loved the world that he gave his one and only Son, that whoever believes in him shall not perish but have eternal life.*

The story (Genesis 3) is known as The Fall of Man or simply '**The Fall**'. The idea that all people are born with a natural inclination to do wrong is called '**Original Sin**'. Christians have different beliefs about Original Sin. Some believe that all humans are born already contaminated by Original Sin. Others see it as a way of showing the weakness of human nature.

The Expulsion from the Garden of Eden by Massacio in the Brancacci chapel of the church Sante Maria del Carmine in Florence, Italy.

ACTIVITIES

Organise a class role-play in a court room where the characters in the story of the Fall are defending themselves against the accusation that they were responsible for bringing evil and suffering into the world. Read the story carefully and work in groups to prepare the case for Adam, Eve, the serpent and God. Appoint a judge and jury to decide who is guilty.

The problem of evil

The next two pages will help you to:

- explain the concepts of natural and moral evil
- evaluate beliefs about why there is evil and suffering in the world
- identify some ways Christians respond to the problem of suffering.

AO1 skills **ACTIVITIES**

Make a list of all the evil things you can think of and create a Venn diagram with one circle for natural evil and one for moral evil. Some things on your list may have elements of both types of evil. Place these in the central, overlapping section. Compare your diagrams and discuss any differences in your classifications.

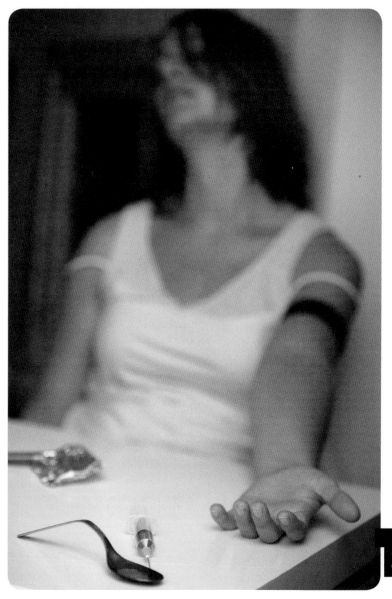

Drug addiction could be seen as an example of moral evil.

Natural and moral evil

Some people believe evil and suffering are either the result of **natural evil** or **moral evil**. Natural evil refers to the suffering and harm resulting from natural events rather than through the actions of humans, for example the physical pain of childbirth, the effects of natural disasters such as earthquakes and tidal waves. Moral evil results from the deliberate, wicked actions of human beings, for example rape, murder, bullying.

How do Christians explain evil and suffering?

The 2nd-century theologian Irenaeus argued that God put evil and suffering into the world for a reason, to enable us to exercise our freedom and develop as human beings. The 20th century theologian John Hick builds on this view, arguing that evil and suffering bring out the best in people and that they are necessary if humans are to develop the qualities of courage, love, selflessness, generosity and compassion. These arguments are called theodicies.

Some people challenge the views of Irenaeus and Hick by asking 'What about severely disabled people or tiny babies who cannot make any sense of their suffering in order to benefit from the experience?'

Other Christians argue that God shares the sufferings of the world because he himself suffered through the death of Jesus. The belief in the incarnation means that the suffering of Jesus was also the suffering of God.

Responses to the problem of suffering

Christians believe they have a responsibility to care for those in need whatever the cause of their suffering. Victims of natural disasters such as droughts or floods depend on others to help them. Many Christians work as volunteers for organisations such as Oxfam, or give money regularly to support charities. They remember the teaching of Jesus in the parable of the Good Samaritan (Luke 10:25–37) that they should love their neighbour; and the message of the parable of the Sheep and the Goats (Matthew 25) that whatever they are doing to help someone in need they are doing for Jesus.

Christians try to show compassion even when suffering is the result of human wickedness. One example of someone who put this into practice was Gordon Wilson whose daughter, Marie, was killed when a bomb exploded in Enniskillen, Northern Ireland on 8 November 1987. The same evening in a television interview Gordon said, '…we have lost a daughter and we shall miss her. But I bear no ill will. I bear no grudge. Dirty sort of talk is not going to bring her back to life. She was a great wee lassie. She loved her profession. She was a pet. She's dead. She's in heaven and we shall meet again. I will pray for these men tonight and every night.'

REMEMBER THIS

You can find more information on the incarnation in Topics 1 and 5.

RESEARCH NOTE

Find out more about the thinking of Irenaeus and John Hick and how theodicies work.

REMEMBER THIS

Refresh your memory by reading the parable of The Sheep and the Goats in Matthew 25 and referring to Topic 3.3 for further information.

RESEARCH NOTE

Find out more about Gordon Wilson and how he spent the rest of his life working for peace and reconciliation in Northern Ireland.

ACTIVITIES

Discuss how an event like Hurricane Katrina might test the faith of a Christian and how he/she might respond?

Plan and role-play a conversation between two people: the first person is a Christian who thanked God for saving him from the hurricane and the second person is his neighbour who has lost her house and everything she owns in the hurricane and believes that it is God's fault.

Coping with suffering

The next two pages will help you to:

- explore Christian responses to coping with suffering
- analyse the story of Job and evaluate its significance for Christians
- reflect on and evaluate your own responses to suffering.

'Satan Smiting Job with Sore Boils' by William Blake, 1825.

RESEARCH NOTE

Find out about the artist and poet William Blake and explore some of the other illustrations he created for the Book of Job.

How do Christians respond to and cope with suffering?

Christians have different ways of explaining and coming to terms with suffering:

- Suffering is a test from God to see how much people trust that in him.
- Suffering leads people to a deeper understanding of God.
- Suffering gives people the opportunity to care for those who are suffering and act in a Christian way.
- Suffering is brought about by humans.
- Suffering is the result of evil and is not caused by God.
- Suffering will not last because it will end with death and life in heaven.

AO1 skills ACTIVITIES

Put the responses to suffering in the list on the left in order from the 'most convincing' to the 'least convincing'. Explain your reasons.

Write your own explanation for the existence of suffering.

The story of Job

The story of Job in the Old Testament is seen by many Christians as an example of how God allows apparently good and innocent people to suffer, perhaps as a test of their faith.

Job, the hero, is described as a perfect and honest man who respects God and avoids evil. He is rich and powerful, with many servants and possessions, and lives happily, surrounded by his family of seven sons and three daughters. Then **Satan** appears on the scene. He tells God that it is easy for Job to be God-fearing when he enjoys every blessing the world has to offer. He throws down a challenge to God saying that if he can threaten Job's prosperity he can soon make him lose his trust in God. God agrees provided that he does not harm Job physically.

Satan destroys everything in Job's life. He is robbed of his possessions. His servants and his sons and daughters are all killed. Despite this Job keeps his trust in God, saying: 'The Lord gives and the Lord has taken away; May the name of the Lord be praised' (Job 1:21b). God then gives Satan permission to cause Job terrible physical suffering so long as he does not kill him. Satan gives Job boils all over his body until he is in so much pain he curses the day he was born.

Three of Job's friends arrive to comfort him but they fail and Job turns on them accusing them of preaching empty words to him, saying 'How long will you torment me and crush me with words?' He feels he has been treated unfairly listing all the good things he has done in his life, asking what he has done to deserve his terrible fate. His comforters accuse Job of daring to question the actions of God, the creator of the universe.

Eventually, after a dramatic encounter with God who speaks to Job out of a storm, Job recognises God's omnipotence and omniscience and repents in dust and ashes. God stops testing him and rewards him. He ends up twice as rich as before with seven new sons and three new daughters and lives to be 140.

Job kept his faith in God even though he was tested by Satan: 'Though he slay me, yet will I hope in him' (Job 13:15a).

Many Christians use the example of the story of Job to support their view that people should not expect to understand why God allows suffering. They should simply accept that they are much smaller than God, and should respond to any troubles with acceptance and faith.

How does faith help Christians cope with suffering?

Faith in God and the example of the suffering of Jesus helps most Christians to cope with suffering. They believe the Bible which promises that they will be rewarded for their faith and courage after death. In his letter to the Christians in Rome, who were suffering persecution for their faith, St Paul wrote 'I consider that our present sufferings are not worth comparing with the glory that will be revealed in us' (Romans 8:18). The Book of Revelation promises people who suffer 'Never again will they hunger; never again will they thirst… And God will wipe away every tear from their eyes' (Revelation 7:16a, 17b).

AO2 skills **ACTIVITIES**

However bad a person's suffering may be, it will end with death and a reward from God.' How might this idea help a Christian to cope with suffering?

What is your own view on this response to suffering?

Sources and reasons for moral behaviour

The next two pages will help you to:

- explain how and why the Bible is a source of moral authority for Christians
- explain the significance of faith in Christ
- evaluate the role of conscience in guiding moral actions
- identify and reflect on sources of authority in your own life.

What helps Christians know right from wrong?

Christians believe that they are created in the image of God and they try to live in ways that would please him. This means doing the right thing and avoiding doing things that are wrong. How do they know what is right and what is wrong?

The authority of the Bible

Christians often study the teachings in the Bible to help them know what is right and what is wrong and how they should act in a particular situation. It is sometimes difficult for Christians to apply the teachings of the Bible to modern-day experiences. It is possible to find passages which could be used to justify most kinds of behaviour. Here,

Christians often turn to the Bible to help them decide what is the right action to take.

AO1 skills ACTIVITIES

Work with a partner to create a mind map around the phrase *moral behaviour*. Include all the things which might influence how someone behaves, laws, school rules, religious texts, rules set by parents, for example. Share your work and use it to build up a class mind map.

the theologian Michael Hampson explains this problem:

❝ *The bible is a hugely diverse collection, the work of hundreds of writers and compilers across more than a thousand years who argue with each other and contradict each other as they apply their own limited human resources to the task of describing the great mystery which is God.* **❞**

(God without God: Western Spirituality without the Wrathful King, Michael Hampson)

The principles which guide Christians in deciding how they should live are based on their belief that God is perfectly good and that, as people were created 'in the image of God' (Genesis 1:27), they share his goodness. Christians follow moral rules, which they believe were given by God, to help them judge between right and wrong. Many Christians see the Ten Commandments as providing the basis for people to live together in harmony.

Faith in Christ

The most important principle which guides Christians in making moral decisions is their faith in Jesus Christ. To help them work out how they should act in particular situations Christians often ask the question, 'What would Jesus have done?' They refer to his teaching that everything can be summed up in a single law of love which is expressed in compassion, forgiveness and even love of your enemies.

Jesus taught people to 'do to others what you would have them do to you' (Matthew: 7:12a). This is sometimes called the 'Golden Rule' and considered by many people, both religious and secular, to be all that is required to live a moral life.

Jesus put this principle into practice in his own life, caring for people who had been rejected and people classed as sinners by society, forgiving his enemies. As he was dying on the cross Jesus asked God to forgive those who had crucified them: 'Father, forgive them for they do not know what they are doing' (Luke 23:34).

Some Christians believe that people will be rewarded for their good actions after death and that people who have done wrong will be punished.

Conscience: deciding for yourself

St Thomas Aquinas taught that conscience was having the requirements of God's law written within your heart. Many people believe that their conscience tells them whether they have done right or wrong, even if no one else knows what they have done. Sometimes they may want to do something but their conscience may prevent them. Some Christians interpret this as God speaking to them. Others think that our conscience depends on the values we have been taught by our parents.

ACTIVITIES

If it was proved that there was no God would that mean everything was morally allowed? Work in small groups to make a list of reasons why people should do good and not evil. Compare your lists as a class and agree a class list.

Ephesians 4:32
Be kind and compassionate to one another, forgiving each other, just as in Christ God forgave you.

Matthew 8:38, 44
You have heard that it was said, 'Eye for eye, and tooth for tooth'… But I tell you: Love your enemies and pray for those who persecute you.

REMEMBER THIS

Look again at the parable of The Sheep and the Goats in Matthew 25 and its importance for how people should behave.

MUST THINK ABOUT!

Have you ever had a guilty conscience about something you've done? How did you feel?

Remember and Reflect

The questions in this section are based on the work you have done throughout this Topic. Try to complete as many questions as you can.

The questions in set 1 are designed to test your factual recall and AO1 level skills (knowledge and understanding). The page numbers alongside the questions will help you to find information that might be useful for your answers. Use them to check against what you have written.

The questions in set 2 are more challenging, using AO2 level skills (use of evidence and reasoned argument to evaluate personal responses and differing viewpoints). Your answers many come from more than one part of the Topic.

AO1 Describe, explain and analyse, using knowledge and understanding

Find the answer on:

1 Explain what each of the following key words means. Use one sentence for each word:
   a moral evil
   b theodicies
   c conscience
   d omnipotent
   e the Devil
   f omniscient

PAGE 44

2 What is meant by Original Sin?

PAGE 44

3 What is meant by The Fall and where in the Bible would you find the story of The Fall?

PAGE 47

4 Who are the four main 'characters' in the story of The Fall?

PAGE 47

5 Explain where a Christian might look for guidance on the right way to behave.

PAGE 52, 53

6 What is the main theme of the story of Job? What does it teach Christians about suffering?

PAGE 51

7 What do people call the kind of evil that is caused by humans doing wrong?

PAGE 48

8 What is meant by natural evil?

PAGE 48

9 Give two examples of natural evil and two examples of moral evil.

PAGE 48

10 Explain three arguments a Christian might give to justify the existence of suffering.

PAGE 49

11 What is the Golden Rule? Do you think it is all that is required to lead a moral life? Give your reasons.

PAGE 53

12 Name two parables of Jesus which help Christians understand how they should treat others.

PAGE 49

13 What did the Devil tempt Jesus to do?

PAGE 47

14 Give an example of a book where good triumphs over evil.

PAGE 47

AO2 Use evidence and reasoned argument to express and evaluate personal responses, informed insights, and differing viewpoints

1 How might a Christian respond to the question 'Why does God allow bad things to happen to good people'?

2 Do you agree with the Christian belief that all people are born sinful?

3 Do you believe in the Devil? Why or why not?

4 Do you think that it is acceptable to say that 'Anything goes' or are there some things which we, as human beings, should condemn in a civilised society? What would those things be in your view?

5 What is the greatest moral evil the world has seen? Think about this question and then share your ideas. Now think about what the greatest moral good might be.

6 'The existence of evil and suffering in the world proves that there is no God.' Do you agree? Give reasons or evidence for your answer, showing that you have thought of more than one point of view. Include reference to Christian beliefs in your answer.

7 Do a survey to find out what people believe about evil. Ask five people you know, but not students in your class, the following questions:

Do you think evil exists?

If yes, what causes evil? If not, why not?

Copy the chart below and use it to record your findings.

Person	Do you think evil exists?	If yes, what causes evil?	If not, why not?
1			
2			
3			
4			
5			

GradeStudio

Welcome to the Grade Studio

Grade Studio is here to help you improve your answers by working through typical questions you might find on an examination paper. For a full explanation of how this feature works and how exam questions are structured, see page 14. For a full explanation of Assessment Objectives and Levels of Response, see pages x–xi in the Introduction.

AO1 Question

How might Christians explain the problem of evil in the world?   [6 marks]

Student's answer

Christians might say that there are both good and evil in the world. Good things come from God and evil things come from the Devil. Some Christians might say that there is evil in the world because many people are evil and they cause this. Other Christians might say that, although God is good, there is so much evil in the world that God cannot stop all of it.

Comments

The candidate has given a satisfactory answer to the question. There are three relevant points but none of them is explained in any detail. The answer needs to give more information and examples in order to reach Level 3. The candidate could also use more technical terms from the specification to show the breadth of their knowledge and understanding.

Student's improved answer

Christians might say that there is both good and evil in the world. Good things come from God and evil things come from the Devil. Some Christians might say that there is evil in the world because many people are evil and they cause this. Other Christians might say that although God is good, there is so much evil in the world that God cannot stop all of it.

Some Christians might say that there is a difference between moral evil and natural evil. Moral evil is caused by human beings, and it is part of our life on earth to work against this evil in order to show God our love. There are some people who believe that natural evil, such as volcanic eruptions, is the work of the Devil.

Others may say that there is evil in the world because humans introduced it when Eve took the fruit from the Tree of the Knowledge of Good and Evil. This introduced Original Sin and it is only because Jesus sacrificed his life that people are not still being punished.

Comments

This is now a good answer to the question. The candidate has shown a clear understanding of the question. There is good description and explanation of a variety of different ways in which Christians might try to understand the existence of good and evil. The candidate has also shown some analysis in dealing with the question of Original Sin. The information is presented clearly and there is good use of technical terms.

AO2 Question

'It is God who makes people suffer.' Discuss this statement. You should include different, supported points of view and a personal viewpoint. You must refer to Christianity in your answer. **[12 marks]**

Student's answer

Christians might disagree with this statement very strongly and say that God is good so God would not let people suffer. Some Christians might say that although God may not always stop suffering, it is not God who causes suffering.

Comments

The candidate has given a limited answer to the question. It is a good beginning to an answer but does not go far enough. There are two relevant points but the candidate now needs to address an alternative view as well as giving their own opinion.

Student's improved answer

Christians might disagree with this statement very strongly and say that God is good so God would not let people suffer. Some Christians might say that although God may not always stop suffering, it is not God who causes suffering.

Some people, on the other hand, might think that because of the amount of suffering, disease and poverty in the world, there cannot be a God and if there was one then he is not a good God. Some Christians might think that suffering is part of God's plan to make humans stronger and better people. I don't believe that God makes people suffer.

My personal opinion is that if there is a God and if this God is good then God would not cause suffering. The fact that there is so much suffering in the world makes me think that God probably does not exist.

Comments

This is now a good answer to the question. The candidate has shown a clear understanding of the question and has presented a range of views supported by evidence and argument. The answer explains Christian views, among others, and includes a personal viewpoint, which is also supported.

These specimen answers provide an outline of how you could construct your response. Space does not allow us to give a full response. You will need to provide more detail in your actual exam responses.

Topic 5: Religion, reason and revelation

The Big Picture

In this Topic, you will be addressing Christian beliefs and teachings about:

- Form and nature of revelation:
  - concept of revelation
  - revelation through mystical and religious experience
  - revelation of God through the world
  - revelation of God in the person of Jesus.
- Authority and importance of sacred texts, looking at:
  - authority of the Bible and reasons for it
  - significance and importance of the Bible.

You will also think about your own feelings and responses to these questions and issues.

DID YOU KNOW?

- Many people have claimed to have personal experiences of God. There are many miraculous events that have occurred in the world that no one can offer a valid explanation for.

- Many Christians believe that God can be experienced by simply looking at the world. They claim it creates feelings of awe and wonder and it is so amazing that only a being such as God could have brought it about.

- The Bible is the best-selling book of all time and has been translated into more than 2000 languages and dialects.

- It is estimated that one in every four people has some form of a religious experience in their lifetime.

Newspapers often use the phrase 'exclusive scoop'. What does this mean and how does it relate to the idea of revelation? Look at some newspaper headlines and explore what they reveal.

Many people believe that they experience God through the beauty of nature.

KEY WORDS

authority The idea that something has power over or can influence people in some way.

conversion A form of religious experience, usually to someone who afterwards changes their beliefs or behaviour.

covenant A special promise or agreement between God and humans.

incarnation God in human form as Jesus on earth.

miracle Something that is amazing and appears to defy the laws of nature, usually attributed to God.

mysticism A form of religious experience where the believer appears unaware of anything except their experience, feelings of unity and peace may be experienced.

numinous Having a sense of being in the presence of the divine.

omnipresence A characteristic of God used to explain he is everywhere.

omniscience A characteristic of God used to describe him as all-knowing.

religious experience An experience of God.

revelation The method through which something is revealed that was previously hidden; in a Christian sense it refers to believers gaining a better understanding of God as he is revealed to them.

Form and nature of revelation (1)

The conversion of Saul (Acts 9).

AO1 skills ACTIVITIES

Think of five questions that you would ask God if it was possible for you to meet and have a conversation with him. Why would you ask these questions? What would you hope to find out about God?

Concept of revelation

Revelation describes how religious believers come to a deeper understanding of God through personal experience, through ways of seeing and experiencing God in the world and through sacred writings. Revelation comes from the word 'reveal' which means to show something that was previously hidden. In this case, God is revealed to Christians in a more meaningful way.

There are many ways to experience God and Christians do not all follow the same paths to bring them closer to God. Christians believe that God wants humans to know him and purposefully reveals himself. He wants to build a relationship with his creation and allow humans to appreciate the world he created for them.

How is God revealed through mystical and religious experience?

Many Christians claim to have undergone direct and personal experiences of God. These experiences often cannot be explained by modern-day science and may only be experienced by individuals. They can raise many unanswered questions and it is difficult to offer proof on either side. There are many types of experiences and some are explained here.

MUST THINK ABOUT!

Do you think religious experiences are real or is there some scientific explanation for them?

Experiencing God through conversion

Conversion is a religious experience that causes a person to change their behaviour or beliefs. One of the best-known examples from the Bible is that of St Paul.

Experiencing God through mysticism

There have been many examples of **mysticism** and mystics within Christianity. Many Christians claim to have felt in the presence of the **numinous**, that is God or the divine. Mystics such as St Teresa of Ávila is one such example. She dedicated her life completely to God and believed in the ascent of the soul where a person becomes one with God and unites with him.

Experiencing God through a miraculous event

Miracles have a long tradition within Christianity. Indeed, Jesus is said to have performed many miracles as explained in the Bible. A **miracle** is an event which appears to defy the laws of nature and cannot be explained. There are many examples of modern miracles when a person may be healed or saved from death. The experience of Bernadette in Lourdes is a famous example of a Christian miracle where she had a vision of the Virgin Mary and a spring appeared at the place where this happened. Many people go on pilgrimage to Lourdes in France to visit this holy and sacred place in the hope that they may be healed.

Experiencing God through worship

God can simply be revealed to Christians through the act of worship. There have been cases where his presence is felt. The Toronto Blessing is one example of this where believers were so overawed by the experience they fell to the floor paralysed, many of them crying. Many Christians feel that God can be experienced through prayer or through reading the Bible in worship.

What impact may these experiences have on a Christian?

The experiences mentioned previously all reveal something about God. He is seen to make a personal and direct connection with them that is seen to deepen faith or even change a person's actions and behaviour completely. Revelation from God that takes the form of religious experience is very special to the individual.

Many Christians believe they have a religious experience every time they pray or worship as they are developing a relationship with God. Any form of contact provides knowledge about God and confirms their faith in him.

Form and nature of revelation (2)

The next two pages will help you to:

- explore the revelation of God through the world and in the person of Jesus
- consider why the revelation of God is important.

AO1 skills ACTIVITIES

Make a list of ten natural things in the world that could have been created by God. What does each of them reveal about him?

Christians believe that God revealed himself to the world through the person of Jesus.

How is God revealed through the world?

Many Christians feel that they can experience God in a meaningful way through the world around us. God is accepted to be the creator of the world and he therefore made everything in it. Christians feel they can experience the presence of God as they walk in the countryside or look at the beauty in nature. It can evoke a sense of awe and wonder which makes them believe that God is close and present within the world.

Christians also accept God as the designer of the world. This suggests an element of thought and planning into the function and purpose of objects within the world. Christians believe that God created the world for them. In the first story of creation in Genesis chapter 1 it says that God created humans last, not only to signify their place in the world but also to show they were his ultimate creation. The world was created for humans and therefore God's power and presence can be seen in everything he created.

Christians believe that the world is too complex and perfect to have been created by chance. When they look at a scientific process such as photosynthesis and the manner in which it works successfully, they argue that is God continuing to act within the world. The human body is a further example of God's creation and people experience the world through their senses. Christians argue that God continues to watch over the world as he has **omniscience** and **omnipresence** which means he is all-knowing and is everywhere.

Christians believe that God created the world for humans to 'rule over'. This is shown with the final part of his creation being humans and humans being made in the image of God, suggesting they are special and more important than other aspects of creation. According to the Bible, God wants to build a relationship with his creation and it is through looking at what he has created for them, that humans can come to know, love and understand God in a more meaningful way.

How is God revealed through the person of Jesus?

Christians believe that the most significant way that God revealed himself to humankind was through the person of Jesus. The **incarnation** (God taking human form) of Jesus showed the depth of his love for his creation and demonstrates his presence and existence. They believe that God cared for his creation and wanted to offer a way for humans to find him. This way was through Jesus.

Nicene Creed

We believe in one Lord, Jesus Christ, the only Son of God, eternally begotten of the Father, God from God, Light from Light, true God from true God, begotten, not made, of one Being with the Father. Through him all things were made. For us men and for our salvation he came down from heaven; by the power of the Holy Spirit he became incarnate of the Virgin Mary, and was made man. For our sake he was crucified under Pontius Pilate; he suffered death and was buried.

Jesus is believed to be the Son of God and this idea makes up part of the Trinity. This is the concept that God is One but understood in three distinct ways – through God as the Father, God as the Son and God as the Holy Spirit. Jesus is God in human form on earth and reveals an aspect of God's nature.

Jesus is held up by Christians as a role model and example to follow. He performed good deeds and helped those he met and Christians believe they should follow his example and try to do the same. Some Christians also believe that they should spread the Word of God just like Jesus did. Jesus therefore, is the ultimate example which Christians aspire to.

God sent his only son to earth in order to show Christians the way he wants them to live their lives. He was willing to sacrifice Jesus for the sins of the world and this demonstrates God's love for humans. It also allows Christians to know and understand God on a deeper level as they appreciate the sacrifice he made for their salvation. God is revealed in human form through the person of Jesus.

FOR DEBATE

'The whole world was created by God and therefore reveals something about him.' Consider this statement. Make a list of arguments for and against it then share your ideas with a partner. Have a class debate to find out what others think.

AO2 skills **ACTIVITIES**

Summarise in your own words what Christians believe about the revelation of God through the world and Jesus. Do you agree with their beliefs? Why or why not?

Authority and importance of sacred texts (1)

The next two pages will help you to:

- explore what the Bible is and what authority it provides
- examine how the Bible is used as a source of authority
- evaluate how relevant the Bible is as a source of authority today.

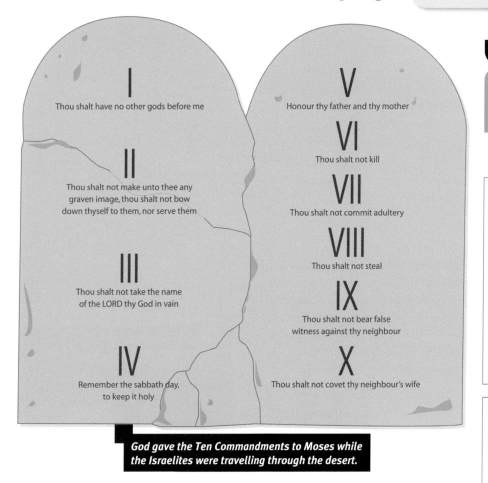

I Thou shalt have no other gods before me	**V** Honour thy father and thy mother
II Thou shalt not make unto thee any graven image, thou shalt not bow down thyself to them, nor serve them	**VI** Thou shalt not kill
	VII Thou shalt not commit adultery
	VIII Thou shalt not steal
III Thou shalt not take the name of the LORD thy God in vain	**IX** Thou shalt not bear false witness against thy neighbour
IV Remember the sabbath day, to keep it holy	**X** Thou shalt not covet thy neighbour's wife

God gave the Ten Commandments to Moses while the Israelites were travelling through the desert.

AO1 skills ACTIVITIES

Think of something that is special to you. Why is it so special? How do you treat it with respect?

The Old Testament
This is the same as the Jewish holy book, the Tenakh. It describes events that took place in the centuries before the coming of Christ and explains how God has been involved in the world over a long period of time. There are 39 books in this section of laws, histories, poems, stories, prophecies and songs.

The New Testament
There are 27 books in the New Testament. Almost all our knowledge about Jesus comes from the New Testament. The first four books are the gospels, a term meaning 'good news'. These are called Matthew, Mark, Luke and John and contain an account of the life, teachings, death and resurrection of Jesus. The remainder of the books contain letters to new churches, history and prophecies about the end of the world. Many Christians feel this is the more important section of the Bible.

What is the Bible?

The Bible is the holy book for Christians. The word 'Bible' comes from a Greek word meaning 'the books'. This is important in understanding what the Bible contains. It is not simply one book but is a collection of many books. It is believed to contain the words of God and is considered to be a form of **revelation**. It is divided into two sections.

Interpreting the Bible

Although the Bible is the holy book for all Christians and considered to be divinely inspired (comes directly from God), there are many ways in which it can be interpreted and understood.

- Some Christians argue that the Bible is literally true. They believe it came directly from God and everything happened exactly as it states. They argue that for this reason, nothing should be questioned or changed. Literalist Christians believe, for example, that the creation stories contained in Genesis are true exactly as they are written and that God created the world in six 24-hour days.

- Other Christians offer a more liberal attitude towards the Bible. They argue that there are different kinds of truth contained in it. They say that some parts of the Bible can be interpreted literally but sometimes it is the message contained in the words that is more important. Sometimes, Liberal Christians adopt a more mythical or story-like understanding of the Bible arguing that it is the meaning that is gained from the Bible that is more useful than the facts themselves. It offers insights into God and humans.

What authority does the Bible provide?

The Bible is given great respect by all Christians as it contains the words of God. It is used as an important source of **authority**, meaning many Christians will base their lives and beliefs upon what it contains. In fact there are three main sources of authority for Christians: the Bible, the Church and their own conscience or advice from others. The Bible is probably given the greatest emphasis because it is believed to be divinely inspired. If Christians need help or guidance on a particular matter, many will turn to the Bible first.

The Old Testament illustrates how God demonstrated his authority over the world and gave rules and laws for humans to follow. There are various examples in the Bible of God making covenants with people, a **covenant** being a promise. One example of this is the covenant made between Abraham and God where Abraham was promised to be the father of many nations and in return would follow the laws set by God and worship only him. A further covenant is offered in the New Testament to all believers through the sacrifice of Jesus, as everyone can ask for forgiveness from God and enter the Kingdom of Heaven.

Christians use the Bible as a guide on which to base their lives. The Ten Commandments are a source of moral and ethical guidance, giving structure and laws for humans to follow. The first four Commandments focus on God and how to worship him. The remaining six Commandments are about how to live peacefully with other people in society.

> **MUST THINK ABOUT!**
>
> The Bible is made up of 66 books in total – 39 in the Old Testament and 27 in the New Testament. It is considered to be the Word of God.

ACTIVITIES

Read the Ten Commandments. Modernise them by rewriting them in your own words. Remember they are rules so must maintain their authority and respect. How do the Ten Commandments act as a source of authority for Christians? Do you think they are still important today?

Authority and importance of sacred texts (2)

The next two pages will help you to:

- examine why the Bible is important for Christians
- reflect on why Christians place so much importance on using the Bible
- identify and evaluate sources of authority in your life.

AO1 skills ACTIVITIES

Make a list of all the reasons why the Bible is important to Christians. Try to rank them in order of importance. Share your ideas with a partner.

Why is the Bible so important to Christians?

Why is the Bible important for Christians?

The Bible is important to Christians for many reasons, some which have been mentioned previously. They believe it contains the words of God and has **authority** for all Christians. It provides a guide for them to live a Christian life and behave how God wishes. They recognise the fact that the **revelation** of God through the Bible offers them support and structure in their lives. It is used in both public and private worship. Reading the Bible regularly helps to develop a relationship with God and is another form of communication like prayer. Passages from the Bible may be read during Church services and at special occasions such as weddings, baptisms and funerals.

MUST THINK ABOUT!

If the Bible doesn't refer to an issue that is in today's society, does that mean that Christianity has no teaching on it? Sometimes the Bible seems vague so does this lessen its importance and influence for Christians? Discuss this issue with a partner and then feed back your ideas to the class.

Christians may read sections of the Bible on a daily basis in order to understand God's intentions for them. They can also turn to the Bible when they are struggling or in need of help and guidance. Often there is a relevant passage in the Bible which serves as a source of inspiration or offers support and comfort in times of need. They may use the example of Jesus and his teachings to help them determine what to do in difficult situations. The Bible is very important as a source of authority, a guide to life and it brings hope and comfort to Christians. It contains all the main teachings of their religion and they will always show great respect towards it.

Christians believe that the Bible contains insights into God and the lives they should be leading. Jesus is held up in the Bible as an example for all Christians to follow. He is God in human form and the stories in the Bible help to make God more understandable to humans. Christians believe that God speaks to them through the Bible and for this reason, many will seek to base their lives around it. It offers guidance and hope for eternal life with God.

Why do Christians place so much importance on using the Bible?

Christians place significant importance on using the Bible. Christianity is a monotheistic religion that is based around the teachings of the Bible. The Bible is believed to contain the words of God and is therefore not only a guide to life, but also a source of comfort and hope in times of difficultly.

When a Christian reads the Bible, they consider themselves to be communicating with God. It is more than simply a book, it is the truth for how they should live their lives and what God intended for humankind. There are a number of sources of authority in the life of a Christian including the teachings of Church leaders and the rules set down by God.

Daniel

66 I am a Christian and I try to read a passage from the Bible every day. It challenges me to think and reflect on my life and ensure that I am doing what God asks of me. Reading the Bible helps connect me to God. I can read his words and understand him. If I am struggling with a particular issue in my life, the Bible is where I turn. There are always words there that will comfort or help me to decide what to do. I have also attended Bible study groups where I can discuss my faith with others and talk about what passages from the Bible really mean. Sometimes it is difficult to find the right direction that God is pointing me in, but I keep my faith and I know his path for me will be revealed. I feel closer to God by having daily communication with him through his holy book – the Bible. 99

What reasons does Daniel give for reading the Bible on a daily basis? Why is the Bible so important to him?

AO2 skills **ACTIVITIES**

Make a list of all the people or things you are influenced by. How do they influence you? Why are they important to you? Who has authority over you and what impact does this have on your life?

Remember and Reflect

The questions in this section are based on the work you have done throughout this Topic. Try to complete as many questions as you can.

The questions in set 1 are designed to test your factual recall and AO1 level skills (knowledge and understanding). The page numbers alongside the questions will help you to find information that might be useful for your answers. Use them to check against what you have written.

The questions in set 2 are more challenging, using AO2 level skills (use of evidence and reasoned argument to evaluate personal responses and differing viewpoints). Your answers many come from more than one part of the Topic.

AO1 Describe, explain and analyse, using knowledge and understanding

Find the answer on:

1 Explain, using examples where appropriate, what each of the following terms means to a Christian. Give as much detail as possible:
   a *conversion*
   b *covenant*
   c *incarnation*
   d *miracle*
   e *mysticism*
   f *numinous*
   g *omniscience*

PAGE 59

2 Give three ways in which God may reveal himself through the world.

PAGE 60, 61

3 What are the defining characteristics of a conversion experience?

PAGE 61

4 Explain, in your own words, Saul's conversion experience.

PAGE 61

5 Using an example to illustrate your answer, explain how God can be revealed through miracles.

PAGE 61

6 How is God revealed through the person of Jesus?

PAGE 63

7 Explain why the Bible is actually a collection of books rather than simply one book.

PAGE 64

8 How many books are there in the:
   a *Old Testament*
   b *New Testament?*

PAGE 64

9 Explain what the Old Testament and the New Testament contain. Try to use examples to explain your answer.

PAGE 64

10 Explain two ways in which the Bible may be understood or interpreted by Christians. Try to give an example for each.

PAGE 65

11 Give three reasons why the Bible is a source of authority for Christians.

PAGE 65–67

12 Explain what a covenant is and give two examples in the Bible.

PAGE 65

13 Why are the Ten Commandments important to Christians?

PAGE 65

14 Write a paragraph showing you understand the rules and ideas contained in the Ten Commandments. PAGE 65

15 Give two reasons why the Bible is important to Christians. PAGE 66

16 Give two examples of how the Bible may be used by Christians. PAGE 67

17 Why do Christians place so much importance on the Bible? PAGE 66

18 Why do Christians place so much importance on using the Bible? PAGE 67

AO2 Use evidence and reasoned argument to express and evaluate personal responses, informed insights, and differing viewpoints

1 Explain your opinion on each of the following statements:
a 'The Bible is a good book to live your life by.'
b 'There is no real evidence of God in the world around us.'
c 'We can't prove if Jesus was a real person so how do we know God was revealing himself?'
d 'There is no point reading the Bible today as it has no relevance to life and issues in today's modern society.'

2 Read through the Ten Commandments. How easy do you think it is to maintain each of these today? Explain your answer.

3 Create a mind map to summarise all the information in this topic. Use words and images and try to illustrate all the key areas.

4 Complete the following table, showing what a Christian would believe and what you believe. If possible try to show what different types of Christians might say.

Topic	Christian view	Your opinion
The interpretation of the Bible	Literalist Christians would argue... Liberal Christians would argue...	I believe...
The revelation of God through miracles	Christians believe...	I think...
The value and authority of the Bible today	Some Christians believe... Other Christians think...	I believe...

GradeStudio

Welcome to the Grade Studio

Grade Studio is here to help you improve your answers by working through typical questions you might find on an examination paper. For a full explanation of how this feature works and how exam questions are structured, see page 14. For a full explanation of Assessment Objectives and Levels of Response, see pages x–xi in the Introduction.

AO1 Question

Explain the importance for Christians of their sacred texts. **[6 marks]**

Student's answer

Christians believe that the Bible is the word of God. This means that it is important because every word in it comes direct from God and so must be the truth.

Some Christians believe that the Bible is important because it was inspired by God but written down by humans and that therefore different parts of the Bible might be truer than others. Some Christians use the Bible as a sort of moral guidebook.

Comments

The candidate has given a satisfactory answer to the question. There are several relevant points but none are dealt with in any detail. The answer needs to give more information and examples in order to reach Level 3. The candidate could also use more technical terms from the specification to show the breadth of their knowledge and understanding.

Student's improved answer

Christians believe that the Bible is the word of God. This means that it is important because every word in it comes direct from God and so must be the truth.

Some Christians believe that the Bible is important because it was inspired by God but written down by humans and that therefore different parts of the Bible might be truer than others. Some Christians use the Bible as a sort of moral guidebook.

Other reasons which Christians might give in support of the importance they attach to the scriptures is that they read the Bible on a regular basis and refer to it when they have difficulties in their lives. They find its words comforting or they give them strength to live a truly Christian life. The Bible can also give people encouragement and hope for the future because they believe it is the word of God and a revealed text, therefore it is more important than other books. So when it promises that Christians will be rewarded for their faith in heaven, they know this is true.

Comments

This is now a good answer to the question. The candidate has shown a clear understanding of the question. There is good description and explanation of a variety of different reasons why the Bible is so important to Christians. The candidate has shown some analysis in dealing with the interpretation of the Bible. The information is presented clearly and there is good use of technical terms.

AO2 Question

'Sacred texts are too old to be useful.' Discuss this statement. You should include different, supported points of view and a personal viewpoint. You must refer to Christianity in your answer. **[12 marks]**

Student's answer

Christians might say that because the Bible is the word of God it does not matter how old it is: it will always be the same. Because the text of the Bible is God's word revealed to humans it will always be useful and important for all time and it will always be able to provide an answer to people's questions about how to live and what to believe.

Comments

The candidate has given a limited answer to the question. There are two relevant points but they both address the same point of view and neither is expanded. The answer needs to give alternative viewpoints, and to include a personal response to reach Level 4.

Student's improved answer

Christians might say that because the Bible is the word of God it does not matter how old it is: it will always be the same. Because the text of the Bible is God's word revealed to humans it will always be useful and important for all time and it will always be able to provide an answer to people's questions about how to live and what to believe.

Some people, on the other hand, might think that because of the age of the Bible it has very little to say about modern issues and problems such as euthanasia and fertility treatment. However, other Christians would say that the Bible contains general teachings and the life and example of Jesus, which would all help people to make decisions. They just need to be applied to new situations. My personal opinion is that the question about whether the Bible is useful depends on whether you believe it is the word of God.

If you do, then you will be able to find answers in it to your questions about how to behave and what God has planned for you. It must be the most important book for you, because it is the inspired word of God. However, if, like me, you are an atheist, then the Bible is just an interesting but very old book with some good ideas, but but it does not help me in my life because it is out of date.

Comments

This is now a good answer to the question. The candidate has shown a clear understanding of the question and has presented a range of views supported by evidence and argument. The answer explains Christian views, among others, and includes a personal viewpoint, which is also supported.

These specimen answers provide an outline of how you could construct your response. Space does not allow us to give a full response. You will need to provide more detail in your actual exam responses.

Topic 6: Religion and science

The Big Picture

In this Topic, you will be addressing Christian beliefs and teachings about:

- the origins of the world and life
- people and animals
- environmental issues.

- Up until medieval times, some people believed that the world was flat. Even in the medieval world, many claimed that the earth was the planet at the centre of the universe and the sun circled around it.

- There are between 1 million and 2 million different kinds of animals alive today.

- Humans have already caused so much damage and destruction to the environment that many people believe that environmental damage is the greatest threat facing society today.

KEY WORDS

Big Bang A scientific theory that a cosmic explosion caused the world to exist.

creation The act of creating something or the thing that is made, in the Bible, the making of the world by God.

Creationists/Literalists A name given to Christians who interpret the Bible literally and accept every word of the Genesis creation story as literally true.

dominion The idea that humans have control over or responsibility for the earth.

evolution The way in which animals and plants adapt to their surroundings – the survival of the fittest.

ex nihilo A Latin term relating to the creation story meaning the universe was created out of nothing.

Genesis The first book of the Bible which contains the stories of creation.

humanity Caring and showing kindness to others, often a term used for all humans.

Non-literalist A name given to a Christian who interprets the Bible as more of a story than literalists and believes it contains important truths but is not a factual account.

stewardship The God-given right or responsibility to care for and manage the world.

'The Thinker' – a statue By Auguste Rodin – is often used to represent philosophy.

The origins of the world and life (1)

The next two pages will help you to:

- explore scientific theories about the origins of the world
- explore Christian beliefs about the origin of the world and life
- evaluate your own views about the origin of the universe.

The Milky Way.

AO1 skills **ACTIVITIES**

How do you think the world started? Make a list of all the possible explanations you can think of. Share them with a partner and see what ideas they came up with. Rank the ideas in order of most probable to least probable.

What theories do scientists have about the origins of the world?

Where did the universe come from? is a question that has puzzled people throughout history. In the past, very little was known about how the world was first formed or how humans came to be on the earth. Ideas and theories put forward were often linked to the religious beliefs of the time. Modern Science has helped to shape views about the origin of the earth and allow scientific theories to be developed, which often contradict those offered by religion. As more has been discovered about the world humans live in, scientific ideas have often replaced those offered by religion.

The study of the universe is known as cosmology. Over centuries, scientists have concluded that the world is much older than previously thought. Today, it is estimated to be 15 and 20 billion years old.

The Big Bang theory

The best-known scientific theory of how the world began is the **Big Bang** theory. This states that around fifteen billion years ago there was a cosmic explosion – a 'big bang' – that caused matter and gases to fly out in all directions. All the universes were formed from this and as the gases cooled, the stars and planets, including earth, took shape.

Evolution

Charles Darwin is well known for his theory of **evolution**, contained in his book *On the Origin of Species.* During the 19th century Darwin observed animals and identified they appeared to have adapted to their environments. His theory of natural selection states that over millions of years plant and animal life adapted to their surroundings and were not created in the form we see them today.

As conditions have changed, for example the climate becoming warmer or colder, some of the characteristics of animals and plants helped them to survive and others did not. This is a process called natural selection where animals and plants with the characteristics best suited to the environment live and the others naturally die out.

Darwin believed humans had evolved over time, the same as plants and animals, rather than being in existence from the beginning of the world. Humans are a higher advanced form of life and he believed they had evolved from the original simpler forms of life. Many people were shocked by Darwin's ideas that humans had evolved from other species whilst others believed his ideas were ridiculous and ridiculed him for them.

What do Christians believe about the origins of the world and humans?

The first book of the Bible is **Genesis** and is where the Christian stories of **creation** are found. The word 'Genesis' means origin and it states that God created the world **ex nihilo**, meaning 'out of nothing'. Genesis mentions six days of creation in which different aspects of the universe were created.

- Day 1: night and day.
- Day 2: sky and water.
- Day 3: land and vegetation.
- Day 4: sun, moon and stars.
- Day 5: creatures of the sea and sky.
- Day 6: other living creatures and humans.

Genesis states that when God had finished, he looked at everything he had created and was pleased with it. On the seventh day, God rested. There are some important religious truths that can be understood from Genesis. These include the fact that God planned the creation of the world and made it for humans to live in. Nothing was created by chance; it was all intended by God to be as he created it.

Christians believe God created humans last in order to show their importance and demonstrate that they were in charge of his creation, an idea known as **dominion**. The Bible states that God 'created man in his own image', suggesting humans are different from animals. Humans were given the duty of **stewardship**. This is a responsibility to look after and care for the world and being a steward is an important role. Christians understand this to mean that their duty is to care for the world as it is only on loan from God and one day they will have to account their actions to him.

> **Genesis 1:1**
>
> *In the beginning God created the heavens and the earth.*

ACTIVITIES

Look carefully at the views of the origin of the world and humanity offered by science and religion. Make a list of any similarities and differences between them. You may like to show your ideas in a table, separating it into 'creation of the world' and 'creation of humanity'.

The origins of the world and life (2)

The next two pages will help you to:

- understand how Christians interpret the story of creation
- explore the arguments between the scientific and Christian views
- evaluate your own views about the relationship between religion and science.

How do Christians interpret the stories of creation?

There are different ways of interpreting Genesis. Some Christians believe aspects of the Bible need to be reinterpreted to adapt to modern society. Scientific advancements have also led some Christians to try and bring aspects of religion together with science.

Creationists or Literalists: Some Christians (known as Creationists or Literalists) take the Bible literally; believing what it states word for word is true. They believe the universe was created in six days, that all living things existed from the beginning of the world and that each 'day' mentioned in Genesis was actually 24 hours. They also reject all scientific discoveries such as the **Big Bang** and **evolution** as they are not mentioned in the Biblical accounts. In the 19th century, Philip Gosse, a naturalist, even suggested that fossil remains found on earth had been put there as a test of faith by God.

Non-Literalists: In contrast, other Christians accept a more liberal approach. They believe that the Genesis creation stories should be understood in a mythical sense. They claim they provide important information but are stories and not factually accurate. They interpret the 'days' of creation to be 'periods of time' and not literally 24 hours. They maintain God created the universe but see no real conflict between science and religion, believing together they give an accurate picture of life. As they accept periods of creation, they are more open to scientific theories such as evolution and the Big Bang.

Intelligent Design: One philosophical theory accepted by some Christians is that of Intelligent Design. This is the theory that the universe is best explained by the existence of an intelligent designer who planned and created it.

The seven days of Creation.

REMEMBER THIS

Think back to the first creation story contained in the Book of Genesis. What was created on each day?

AO1 skills ACTIVITIES

Create a table summarising the main views of each of the following theories: creationists or literalists; non-literalists/liberalists; Intelligent Design.

Whichever Christian interpretation is accepted, there are some important points about Christian belief to note:

- The creation of the world and life was not an accident but intended.
- God created the world and everything in it for a purpose.
- The world was created perfect.
- Humans were created in the 'image of God' and given responsibilities within the world.

Are science and religion in conflict?

Many people believe science and religion are in conflict over issues such as the creation of the universe. They argue they present different theories about where the universe came from and cannot agree. Others believe that together they provide a complete picture and answer to challenging questions such as 'Where did the universe come from?'

Some people argue that science gives facts because it is a discipline based on using evidence and performing experiments which can prove whether something is true or not. In contrast, religion tries to look at the purpose or reasons behind something as it focuses on why things happen rather than providing empirical evidence. The table below summarises these different approaches.

Religion	Science
Asks WHY questions.	Asks HOW questions.
Tries to explain the purpose of things.	Tries to show how things happen – uses facts.
Explains value and importance.	Explains processes and methods.
Based on sacred writings such as the Bible, personal experiences and tradition.	Based on knowledge and hypotheses.
Not open to scientific testing.	Open to review as ideas change and more evidence becomes available.
Can be taken literally but often interpreted as more story like, containing important truths.	Taken as explanations of how things happen.

Some atheists, however, have argued that the reason the universe seems designed for humans is simply because humanity has evolved to live in its conditions:

66 *Imagine a puddle waking up one morning and thinking, 'This is an interesting world I find myself in, an interesting hole I find myself in, fits me rather neatly, doesn't it? In fact it fits me staggeringly well, must have been made to have me in it!' This is such a powerful idea that as the sun rises in the sky and the air heats up and as, gradually, the puddle gets smaller and smaller, it's still frantically hanging on to the notion that everything's going to be alright, because this world was meant to have him in it, was built to have him in it; so the moment he disappears catches him rather by surprise. I think this may be something we need to be on the watch out for.* **99**

Douglas Adams, from a speech given at Digital Biota 2, Cambridge, September 1998

AO2 skills **ACTIVITIES**

'The creation stories are fiction, science must be right.' Discuss this statement. You should include different, supported points of view and a personal viewpoint. You must refer to Christianity in your answer.

People and animals

The next two pages will help you to:

- explore the relationship of humanity and animals according to Christians
- explain Christian views about the treatment of animals.

Should animals have the same rights as humans?

What do Christians believe about animals?

Christians see animals as part of God's **creation**. According to the first **Genesis** story of creation, they were made before humans and it is part of human responsibility as stewards to look after and care for them. In Genesis it states that Adam was given responsibility by God to name the animals and is told to rule over them. What this actually means has led to some debate but it seems that humans are expected to act as caretakers of animals.

Much of the debate surrounding the issues of animals is related to how a passage of the Bible is interpreted. Genesis 1:27–28 talks about humans 'ruling over' the animals and some may interpret this to mean humans are better and have power over the animals whilst others feel it is alluding to **stewardship** where humans should look after the animals. **Dominion** is also important. This relates to the idea that humans have control over or responsibility for the earth and everything on it, including animals.

AO1 skills **ACTIVITIES**

Make a list of all the ways in which humans use animals, for example for food. Then share your ideas with a partner and rank them in order of acceptability.

 **REMEMBER THIS**

The word stewardship is the God-given duty to care for and manage the earth.

What do Christians believe about the relationship between humanity and animals?

The relationship between humanity and animals is often a discussion about whether animals should have any rights. Most Christians accept that humans were given a responsibility from God to look after and care for all animals therefore humans are seen as more important.

Some Christians may argue that as animals are similar to humans they should be given the same rights. For example, animals feel pain just like humans and this should be taken into consideration. However, the main difference seen by Christians between humans and animals is that humans are believed to have a soul. The soul is seen as a divine spark, often the connection between a person and God, and as being unique and distinct to humans. This may be used as an argument to suggest that humans are more important than animals and therefore should rule over the animals.

Roman Catholics believe that animals do not have rights but their teaching focuses on the duties humans have towards animals. They believe animals should be looked after and cared for properly but they are not equal to humans. They therefore would always put human rights above those of animals. They believe that animals are owed respect and appropriate care but if there is a choice to be made about money for example being spent on either humans or animals, human rights should always be given more importance.

Quakers believe that that they should show consideration for all of God's creatures and one aspect of this could be to stand up for the rights of animals. They would try to balance the rights of humans with kindness towards animals and attempt to bring about the good of both.

What do Christians believe about the treatment of animals?

Animals are used in many ways in today's world. They are used for eating, making clothes, for hunting, for forms of entertainment and in medical and cosmetic testing. Often stories are in the media about animals being ill-treated or not cared for properly. Christians hold a variety of views about whether it is acceptable to use animals for human gain.

Most Christians feel it is acceptable to use animals for food although are concerned that they are killed humanely and not caused unnecessary pain. Some Christians, however, may feel that they were given the role from God to look after and care for animals and so become vegetarians.

Many Christians believe they have a responsibility to care for and protect animals and therefore feel it is important to prevent the loss of animal habitats, unnecessary killings and cosmetic testing on animals. Some Christians would argue that medical testing which helps humans is acceptable as the results of this benefit human development and knowledge but cosmetic testing on animals is unacceptable as this is not necessary for human survival.

MUST THINK ABOUT!

Are humans and animals the same? Should animals be treated the same or differently from humans? Why?

 **ACTIVITIES**

Make a list of arguments for animals having rights and arguments against animals having rights. Use your lists to help you answer the following question: 'Humans will always be more important than animals.' Do you agree?

Environmental issues

What do Christians believe about the environment?

Christians believe that the world and everything in it belongs to God and it is their role and responsibility on earth to care for it. God made the world for humans to 'rule over' but this does not mean humans can do whatever they want to it. Stewardship is the idea that **humanity** was given a responsibility from God to look after and care for the world.

For many Christians their responsibility for the planet means they think they should take action to preserve the environment and not do more damage to it. This is important when looking at God's **creation** as humans have already done much damage to the world.

In the past Christians and humanity in general have not been too concerned about what has been happening to the planet. They have taken an attitude that they will find a solution or that it is not their responsibility to deal with the issue. However, today there is much more awareness of the damage already caused and people look for methods of limiting this and not causing any further harm to the planet.

It is seen as everyone's responsibility to care for the earth and as Christians accept stewardship, it is vital they take this responsibility seriously. Christians believe that part of this responsibility is to make others aware of the situation and encourage everyone to try to help.

The next two pages will help you to:

- explain Christian beliefs and teachings about how they should treat the environment
- explore the concept of stewardship and identify ways in which Christians respond to environmental issues
- evaluate your own views about human responsibility for the environment.

Environmental pollution is not good stewardship.

How might Christians respond to environmental issues?

The planet has already come to much harm because of humans. Pollution, deforestation, damage to habitats, global warming, the destruction of the ozone layer and exhausting the world's natural resources are just a few that can be mentioned. Animals and their habitats have also been destroyed as a knock-on effect from the damage caused to the world.

Many Christians believe that issues such as these need to be addressed if we are to be able to live on the earth for generations to come. Some scientists believe time is running out for the planet and the damage that has already been caused is too bad to change completely.

Christians may do many things to try and respond to environmental issues:

- pray for strength and help in looking after the planet
- recycle items such as cardboard, glass and plastic and encourage others to do the same
- use cars with low emissions or take advantage more of public transport or car sharing
- vote for someone in local elections who promises to try to help the local environment
- become involved in local projects which try to help clean up areas and reverse some of the damage already caused
- raise awareness of the issues that the world faces and the damage already caused and encourage others to do something about it
- use products that are not harmful to the environment
- be less wasteful by turning off lights or not leaving televisions on standby, for example
- join an organisation that works for the good of the environment such as Greenpeace.

Most Christians accept that they must take some responsibility for looking after the environment, especially as it is mostly down to humans that the damage has occurred in the first place. Christians take their responsibility seriously and believe that they must act now in order to help reverse the damage done to the environment and animals. By acting, Christians are showing that they take their duty and responsibility of stewardship seriously and are offering practical help that can try to undo some of the damage already caused to the environment of the world and preserve it for future generations.

ACTIVITIES

In pairs, make a list of all the ways in which the environment of the planet has been damaged. Be as specific as possible. Rank your ideas to show which of them are permanent damage and which humans can help to reverse.

FOR DEBATE

Prepare a debate speech on the statement 'Humans can do whatever they like to the world.' You will need to make a list of arguments for and against this statement. You will also need to include quotes and evidence to support your view and ideas that support the opposite view. You may like to take a vote at the beginning and the end of the debate to see how many students changed their opinion about the statement.

MUST THINK ABOUT!

What can you do to help the environment in your area? Do you think it is important for everyone to become involved in local projects? Why or why not?

ACTIVITIES

How much responsibility do you think humans should take for the damage to the world? Does this mean everyone has a duty to try and help reverse the damage and preserve the environment?

Remember and Reflect

The questions in this section are based on the work you have done throughout this Topic. Try to complete as many questions as you can.

The questions in set 1 are designed to test your factual recall and AO1 level skills (knowledge and understanding). The page numbers alongside the questions will help you to find information that might be useful for your answers. Use them to check against what you have written.

The questions in set 2 are more challenging, using AO2 level skills (use of evidence and reasoned argument to evaluate personal responses and differing viewpoints). Your answers many come from more than one part of the Topic.

AO1 Describe, explain and analyse, using knowledge and understanding

Find the answer on:

1 Explain what each of the following terms means. Write one sentence for each word:
  a creation
  b dominion
  c evolution
  d humanity
  e stewardship

PAGE 72

2 Explain in your own words the scientific theories of the Big Bang and evolution.

PAGE 74, 75

3 Describe each day of creation according to the first Genesis creation story.

PAGE 75

4 Create a Venn diagram showing the main similarities and differences between the literalist/creationist and non-literalist interpretations of the Genesis story of creation.

PAGE 76

5 Give three reasons why many people believe the scientific and religious explanations of creation are in direct conflict with each other.

PAGE 77

6 Explain why science answers 'How?' questions and religion answers 'Why?' questions.

PAGE 77

7 Give an explanation of how science and religion may not actually be seen as being in conflict about the creation of the world.

PAGE 77

8 Explain why there is a debate between some Christians over whether God intended humans to use animals or simply look after them. Try to refer to a Biblical teaching in your answer.

PAGE 78, 79

9 Explain how the concepts of stewardship and dominion apply to humans and animals.

PAGE 78, 79

10 Give a summary of what Christians believe to be the relationship between humans and animals.

PAGE 78, 79

11 Give three ways in which Christians might show care and consideration for all of God's creatures.

PAGE 78, 79

12 Explain why some Christians may be vegetarian.

PAGE 79

13 Give four examples of how humans have already damaged the environment. PAGE 80, 81

14 Why do Christians believe it is important to care for the environment? Try to refer to Christian teachings in your answer. PAGE 80

15 Give six ways in which Christians can try to overcome and help the problems facing the environment. PAGE 81

AO2 Use evidence and reasoned argument to express and evaluate personal responses, informed insights, and differing viewpoints

1 Give your opinion on the following statements, making sure you explain your reasons for your view clearly:
   a 'Religion and science together explain the origins of the world.'
   b 'Animals are there for humans to use as they please.'
   c 'I didn't damage the world so why should I clear up the mess?'
   d 'Animals are useful to test products on so that humans don't get hurt.'

2 Create a multiple answer quiz for this unit. You should aim to test knowledge of key words and ideas as well as religious teachings.

3 Explain the views of a scientist and Christian on each of the following topics and then state your own opinion. Make sure you explain why each person holds different views. You may like to illustrate your ideas in a table to make each view clear:
   a The creation of the world
   b The origin of humanity

4 In the boxes below are some key ideas. Answer the following question, making sure you mention and explain each of the ideas in the boxes:

'The world belongs to humans and therefore they can do what they like to animals and the environment.' Discuss this statement. You should include different, supported points of view and a personal viewpoint. You must refer to Christianity in your answer.

stewardship	rights of the animals
damage already done to the world	dominion
scientific explanations of creation	Big Bang
evolution	Genesis stories of creation
humanity	religious explanations of creation

GradeStudio

Welcome to the Grade Studio

Grade Studio is here to help you improve your answers by working through typical questions you might find on an examination paper. For a full explanation of how this feature works and how exam questions are structured, see page 14. For a full explanation of Assessment Objectives and Levels of Response, see pages x–xi in the Introduction.

AO1 Question

Explain why some Christians might not accept scientific theories about the origins of the world. **[6 marks]**

Student's answer

Student's answer	Comments
Some Christians do not accept scientific theories about the origins of the world because they do not agree with the Biblical accounts in the book of Genesis. Some Christians have worked with Christian scientists to disprove scientific theories such as the Big Bang, and to show that the Biblical accounts are true and that God created the world in six days. People say that if you believe in God then you must believe that the Bible is true, so Christians do not have any alternative but to believe in the Genesis creation accounts.	The candidate has given a satisfactory answer to the question. There are several relevant points but none of them is explained in any detail. The answer needs to give more information and examples in order to reach Level 3. The candidate could also use more technical terms from the specification to show the breadth of their knowledge and understanding.

Student's improved answer

Student's improved answer	Comments
Some Christians do not accept scientific theories about the origins of the world because they do not agree with the Biblical accounts in the book of Genesis. Some Christians have worked with Christian scientists to disprove scientific theories such as the Big Bang, and to show that the Biblical accounts are true and that God created the world in six days. People say that if you believe that God inspired the Bible then you must believe that the Bible is true, so Christians do not have any alternative but to believe in the Genesis creation accounts. Some Christians do not see this as a problem. They believe that the stories of creation in Genesis are myths. This means that they are not literally true in themselves, but that they contain essential truth – in this case, that God created the world. It does not matter whether he did it in 6 days or through the Big Bang and evolution over many years. If Christians accept this view, then scientific theories do not pose a problem. If there was a Big Bang, it was caused by God.	This is now a good answer to the question. The candidate has shown a clear understanding of the question. There is good description and explanation of a variety of different ways in which Christians might respond to scientific theories about the origins of the world. The information is presented clearly and there is good use of technical terms. In addition, the candidate has not written about the origins of humanity and evolution, which are not relevant to the question.

AO2 Question

'The world is ours to treat as we like.' Discuss this statement. You should include different, supported points of view and a personal viewpoint. You must refer to Christianity in your answer.

[12 marks]

Student's answer

Christians might say that God put them on the Earth to look after it and that they have to take care of the world. Some Christians might also say that at the creation of human beings God made them stewards, which means they have a duty to take care of creation.

Comments

The candidate has given a limited answer to the question. There are two relevant points but they both address the same point of view and neither is expanded on. The answer needs to give alternative viewpoints, and also to include a personal response to reach Level 4.

Student's improved answer

Christians might say that God put them on the Earth to look after it and that they have to take care of the world. Some Christians might also say that at the creation of human beings God made them stewards, which means they have a duty to take care of creation.

Some people, on the other hand, might think that people were simply placed on the world, or evolved from animals and that therefore they have no more responsibility than any other life form to take care of it. However, even people with no religious belief might think that they owe a duty to generations to come to make sure that the earth is still habitable. My personal opinion is that all people have a responsibility towards the earth.

I believe this because we all live on it and that, because humans have developed differently from other animals, it is their responsibility to ensure that the Earth and the species on it survive.

Comments

This is now a good answer to the question. The candidate has shown a clear understanding of the question and has presented a range of views supported by evidence and argument. The answer explains Christian views, among others, and includes a personal viewpoint, which is also supported.

These specimen answers provide an outline of how you could construct your response. Space does not allow us to give a full response. You will need to provide more detail in your actual exam responses.

exam**Café**

Welcome to Exam Café

Now you have finished the course/Topic, it is time to revise and prepare for the examination. A key to any exam is the revision and preparation leading up to it. The key to good revision is to 'work smart'. This section will guide you to in knowing what is needed for success and just as important, what is not. So don't panic! Think positive. GCSE is about what you *can* do, not what you can't.

Key points to note at this stage

There are two important points to consider before you begin your revision programme:

1 Your revision will need to focus on what is needed in the answers so that you can achieve the best possible mark. Remember the AO1 and AO2 assessment objectives. Each of these objectives is worth 50 per cent of the total mark.

2 You also need to know that the exam questions on the paper are designed to test your performance with both AO1 and AO2 objectives. Each question will be made up of five parts:

- Four AO1 parts of which three check your knowledge and one tests your understanding and analysis.

- One question testing AO2 – your ability to consider different points of view on a particular issue and how much you can express your own points of view with relevant evidence and argument.

Once you understand what is needed, it will be time to turn to your revision programme.

How to get started

An important key to success with any exam is the preparation beforehand. While few people enjoy the process of revision it is something that is vital for success. Your class teacher will also discuss revision with you. Below are some suggestions and ideas that can be employed:

1 It is vital to revise in plenty of time before the exam. Do not leave everything to the last minute.

2 Design a revision timetable and be realistic about what can be achieved.

3 Revision is a personal matter and we all learn in different ways. Remember that many revision skills can be transferred between different subjects.

4 These are some suggested revision techniques:

   - Create summary cards for each topic – a maximum of 5–10 bullet points on each card.

   - Create lists of key words and terms. Ask somebody to test you on them or hang them around the house.

   - Create a mind map to summarise a major topic.

   - Design cards with a word or idea on one side and a question/ definition or answer on the other. These allow you to be tested by family members or friends who may not have much subject knowledge.

   - Create an A–Z list on a certain topic. This involves writing the 26 letters of the alphabet down the side of a page and then having to write a key word or teaching connected to that topic for each letter of the alphabet.

   - Remember that religious teachings do not have to be learned word-for-word. It is acceptable to paraphrase them.

5 Break your revision sessions of 5–10 minutes to start with (this can be increased as you become much better at it). Give yourself a short break (of about 5 minutes) and then go back to revising. Remember that spending time revising when nothing is going in is as bad as doing no revision at all.

6 Try answering questions on past papers then marking them with the mark scheme yourself. Alternatively, you can write your own questions and develop your own mark scheme. Answer the questions and use the levels of response to mark them.

7 Finally, remember that if you go into revision with a negative attitude you are ultimately going to make it much tougher on yourself.

ExamCafé

Revision
Common errors and mistakes

So the day of the exam has arrived. Remember that you are not the first to sit exams and you will not be the last. However, learn from the experience of others and do not fall into any of the following exam traps:

Misreading the question: Take a minute and read the question carefully. Surprisingly a large number of candidates do not read the questions properly. They simply see a word or miss a point and feel they have to start writing. No matter how good your answer is, if it does not answer the question it will not gain you any marks.

Wasting valuable time: The exam is a race against the clock. Match the length of your response to the number of marks being awarded. A one-mark question can be answered with a single word or a sentence and not a paragraph.

Disorganised waffle: Written answers, especially AO2 style answers, require you to plan your answer thoughtfully. It requires a range of viewpoints including religious responses and your own views. Be careful and do not let your own views take over.

Poor selection of knowledge: Choose good examples that help you to develop and explain your ideas, for example if a question asks you to explain why it is important for Christians to read the Bible, don't just answer 'because their religion requires it'.

It is Religious Studies after all: Remember that the subject is Religious Studies and you will be tested on your knowledge and understanding of religion and its impact on the lives of individuals and communities. Make sure your answers contain relevant religious ideas.

Know the exam paper: Make sure that you fully understand the layout and instructions for the exam paper. In particular focus on which questions you must do and how many questions you are required to do.

Revision checklist

The details of the course are known as the Specification. It is broken down into the Topics listed below. There is a summary of the key areas within each Topic that you need to know about.

TOPIC 1 BELIEF ABOUT DEITY

For this Topic you must:
- know the meaning of all the technical terms in the specification, so you could answer factual questions such as, 'What is meant by the Trinity?'
- know and understand how topics connect, for example beliefs about the existence of God, the nature of God and miracles are all linked.

TOPIC 2 RELIGIOUS AND SPIRITUAL EXPERIENCE

For this Topic you must:
- know about how Christians worship in public and at home, and the way in which art and music are used in worship
- know and be able to explain the technical terms in the specification, such as 'fasting', 'symbolism', 'prayer' and 'meditation'.

TOPIC 3 THE END OF LIFE

For this Topic you must:
- be able to give clear explanations of Christian understandings of body and soul
- be able to explain the technical terms 'heaven', 'hell', 'purgatory', 'salvation' and 'redemption through the suffering of Christ'
- be able to explain the idea of God as a judge
- have good knowledge of Christian funeral ceremonies so that you can explain how they reflect belief and support the bereaved.

TOPIC 4 GOOD AND EVIL

For this Topic you must:
- be able to show understanding of the concepts of good and evil (including natural and moral evil) and the ideas of God and the Devil
- be able to explain the ideas of the Fall, original sin and redemption
- be able to explain how Christians might cope with suffering and the ways in which they decide how to behave morally.

TOPIC 5 RELIGION, REASON AND REVELATION

For this Topic you must:
- be able to give a clear explanation of the concept of revelation and explain revelation through sacred texts as well as through religious experience
- be able to explain the ideas of revelation of God through the world and in the person of Jesus.

TOPIC 6 RELIGION AND SCIENCE

For this Topic you must:
- be able to explain scientific theories about the origins of the world and of humanity
- be able to explain Christian teachings about the origins of the world and of humanity
- be able to explain the relationship between humans and animals
- be able to write about environmental issues and provide Christian responses to these.

ExamCafé

Exam preparation

Sample student answer

Now you have done some serious revision it is time to see what sort of responses you will need to produce to build a better answer. Here are some examples of responses with comments to show you what is good about them and how they could be improved.

Remember examiners will use levels of response for part d which is AO1 and part e which is AO2. For parts a, b and c responses will be point marked. This means that if there is one mark allocated for the question, only one point is expected, if two marks are allocated, then two points are expected and so on. Part a is worth one mark, b two marks and c three marks.

AO1 a-c

This question and example response are from Topic 6 Religion and science.

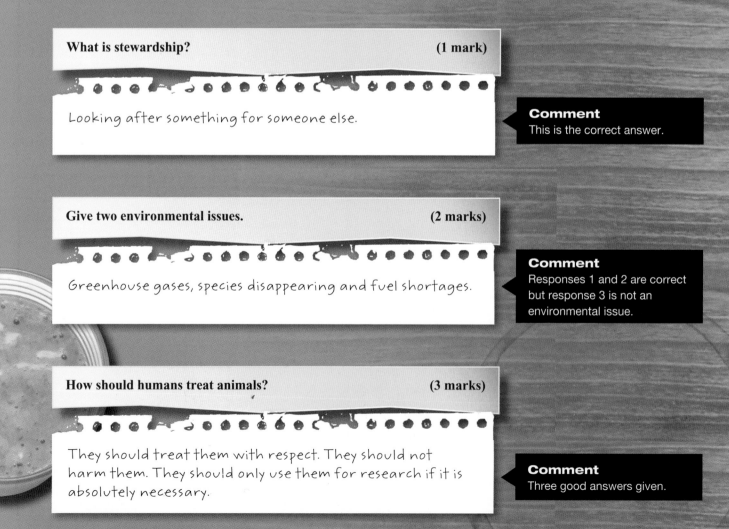

What is stewardship? (1 mark)

Looking after something for someone else.

Comment
This is the correct answer.

Give two environmental issues. (2 marks)

Greenhouse gases, species disappearing and fuel shortages.

Comment
Responses 1 and 2 are correct but response 3 is not an environmental issue.

How should humans treat animals? (3 marks)

They should treat them with respect. They should not harm them. They should only use them for research if it is absolutely necessary.

Comment
Three good answers given.

AO1 Part d questions

Let us look now at some responses to the AO1 part d of a question, which is going to be marked by levels of response. These questions are worth six marks, but this does not mean that you need to produce six points, or three points with some development. You will need to show the depth of understanding in your responses. This could be shown by referring to several points and developing each of them a little, or by developing one or two points fully.

This question and example response are from Topic 4: Good and evil.

> **Explain how Christians might explain why there is evil in the world.**
> **(6 marks)**

Response 1

Christians might say that the reason that there is evil in the world is because it is the work of the Devil. They believe that the Devil was Lucifer, a fallen angel, who disobeyed God and was sent to rule in hell. They believe that the Devil causes people to act badly and against God's wishes, and that this is why there is evil in the world.

Response 2

Christians might say that the reason that there is evil in the world is because it is the work of the Devil. They believe that the Devil was Lucifer, a fallen angel, who disobeyed God and was sent to rule in hell. They believe that the Devil causes people to act badly and against God's wishes, and that this is why there is evil in the world.

Other Christians believe that evil is a natural part of human beings, who are tempted to do evil acts. It is the teachings of the Bible and the love of God that persuade them not to do this. Some Christians might distinguish between moral evil, which is caused by people, and natural evil, which are events such as earthquakes, and which are outside of human control. They might point out that there are still good things in life.

Comment
This is a satisfactory response, reaching Level 2. The information given is relevant, and accurate reasons have been chosen. However, the response is not well developed and is essentially one-sided, giving only one explanation.

Comment
This is a good response. It contains much of the satisfactory 'Response 1' but it is much more developed. The reasons for different views are explained. There is appropriate use of technical language such as moral and natural evil. This response would reach Level 3.

Exam preparation
Sample student answer

AO2

Part e of each question in the exam will involve an AO2 question asking you to explain different points of view about a particular issue. It also gives you an opportunity to present your own personal viewpoint. However, please remember that all viewpoints on a particular issue must be backed up with good evidence, argument and reasoning. Part e of each question is worth 12 marks, or 50 per cent of the total, so it is important to think carefully about how you are going to tackle these questions.

Planning an AO2 answer

These questions want different points of view about a particular issue. Your answer could therefore be structured in the following way:

Paragraph 1: Explain a view which will *agree* with the statement in the question. Offer evidence, beliefs and teachings to back up the point of view.

Paragraph 2: Explain a *different* view from what the statement is suggesting. Again you need to offer evidence, beliefs and teachings to back up your point of view.

Paragraph 3: Include your own personal viewpoint about the issue raised. Again you need to offer evidence, belief and arguments to support your point of view. It does not matter which point of view you take, there is no right or wrong answer. Instead you need to show your ability to reason and argue. If you really do not have a strong point of view on this issue just simply go for the viewpoint that you can best argue.

Below is an example of an AO2 question and the different levels of response from Topic 3: The end of life.

'People believe in heaven because they are afraid of dying.' (12 marks)

Response 1

Lots of people might believe in heaven because they are afraid of dying. Everyone is afraid of dying, and heaven offers a hope that there might be something else after you die. Some people might say that they believe in heaven because it says in the Bible that people will go to heaven.

Comment
This is Level 1. Two relevant viewpoints are stated but there is little support to back them up. This is a simplistic response and shows limited understanding of the question. There is no use of technical terms.

Response 2

Lots of people might believe in heaven because they are afraid of dying. Everyone is afraid of dying, and heaven offers a hope that there might be something else after you die. However, Christians believe in heaven because it says in the Bible that people who trust in Jesus and follow his teachings will go to heaven.

Response 3

Lots of people might believe in heaven because they are afraid of dying. Everyone is afraid of dying, and heaven offers a hope that there might be something else after you die. However, Christians believe in heaven because it says in the Bible that people who trust in Jesus, follow his teachings and accept him as their saviour will go to heaven. There are many church teachings about heaven as well as about hell and purgatory, and it is more likely that people believe in some of these rather than believe in it just because they are afraid. My personal opinion is that I do not believe in life after death because there is no evidence for it.

Response 4

Lots of people might believe in heaven because they are afraid of dying. Everyone is afraid of dying, and heaven offers a hope that there might be something else after you die. However, Christians believe in heaven because it says in the Bible that people who trust in Jesus, follow his teachings and accept him as their saviour will go to heaven. There are many church teachings about heaven as well as about hell and purgatory and it is more likely that people believe in some of these because they follow the teaching of the Church rather than believe in heaven just because they are afraid of dying. My personal opinion is that I do not believe in life after death because there is no evidence for it. No one has ever come back from the dead to tell us about what happens and there is no scientific evidence for believing that there is a heaven or hell. So I am not worried about dying because I know that will be the end.

Comment
This is Level 2. This is a better answer as it explains to the examiner what the candidate understands the question to be about. However, although two viewpoints are stated and slightly developed, the response is still rather limited.

Comment
This is a competent response and meets the criteria for Level 3. It is reasonably well organised and contains some significant views that are explained well and have evidence to justify them. There is a balance of views. There is good use of technical terms. However there is no support for the personal response and this limits the response to Level 3.

Comment
The personal response presents a new view and comes to a conclusion. The candidate has grasped the significance of the issue. The personal view is backed up by evidence. There is good, accurate use of specialist terms and the response is reasonably well organised. This will take the response to Level 4.

ExamCafé

Exam preparation
Understanding exam language

Examiners try to keep questions short and clear. To do this they use special trigger words to hint at how you should respond to the questions. Below is a list of common trigger words. You should familiarise yourself with these words:

State	Usually used in AO1 questions worth 1–3 marks. This means write down a fact about something, for example *State what is meant by the Trinity*.
Give	This is used instead of 'state' and requires the same sort of response.
List	This is used instead of 'give' or 'state' and requires the same sort of response.
Describe	This is used in AO1 questions and means 'tell the examiner factual information about the item or idea'. An example is *Describe what is meant by the Trinity,* which means 'write down factual information about what the Christian belief of the Trinity is'.
Give an account of	This is asking for the same sort of response as 'describe', for example *Give an account of why some Christians fast.*
Explain	This means show that you understand something, for example *Explain what is meant by the Eucharist*. An 'explain' response will include some knowledge, but the best responses will give a range of ideas and reasons.
Why	This word is used as shorthand for 'explain'. Put the word 'explain' in front of it and you will know what to do, for example *Why do many Christians fast?* is the same as *Explain why many Christians fast*.
What	This can be used to ask you for factual information, for example *What happens at a funeral?* It can also be used for questions that are asking for understanding where there is a mixture of fact and understanding required, for example *What is meant by Heaven and Hell?*
Important	This word is used frequently in AO1 part d questions and it indicates that you say why Christians should or should not do/believe something. An example is *Explain why salvation is important to Christians*, which means, *Give reasons to explain why salvation is thought about in a special way in Christianity.*

Examiner Tips
Planning and structuring an answer

In the Grade Studios you have been shown how to build levels of response. This is really important for the AO1 responses to part d worth six marks and the AO2 responses to part e worth 12 marks. In each case follow this structure:

- Check you really know what the question is asking. In the AO2 questions work out the key word or words in the statement, for example *When people die that is the end. Discuss this statement.* The key phrase here is *Discuss this statement.* If the answer does not deal with this, then it will be awarded a low mark.
- Make a note of key points to include all AO1 responses and use a diagram to note down viewpoints for AO2.
- Begin your answer with a brief mention of what the question is asking you to do.
- Write clearly and concisely. DON'T WAFFLE.
- Reach a conclusion at the end of your answer. In the case of an AO1 answer this could be a brief summary sentence, for example *So this shows why salvation is important to many Christians.* In the case of an AO2 answer the conclusion should include a **personal view** (with supporting reasons/argument) and a **brief summing up** of the different views you have expressed.
- Leave a gap of a few lines between each answer. This is in case you wish to add further ideas/information later (if you don't, there is no need to worry).
- If you have any time left at the end of your exam use it constructively. Check your answer makes sense. Check your answer is responding to the question set. Check your use of English, grammar and spelling. Check you have answered the required number of questions. **Remember when you hand in your answer paper at the end of the exam it is probably the last time you will ever see it. Make sure it is your best possible effort.**

Topic 7: Religion and human relationships

The Big Picture

In this Topic, you will be addressing religious beliefs and teachings about:

- the roles of men and women in a Christian family
- marriage and marriage ceremonies
- divorce
- sexual relationships and contraception.

You will also think about the ways in which these beliefs affect the life and outlook of Christians in today's world.

DID YOU KNOW?

- Some Christians accept civil partnerships.
- Faithfulness and commitment are valued highly by Christians.
- Marriage takes place in church but a legal divorce can only take place in court.

KEY WORDS

adultery A married person having a sexual relationship with someone to whom they are not married.

annulment A marriage terminated by the Church because it was not valid.

civil partnership Legal recognition of a same-sex relationship with a registry office ceremony.

commitment A bond between a couple.

divorce The legal ending of a marriage.

pre-marital sex Having a sexual relationship before marriage.

promiscuity Having many sexual partners without commitment.

re-marriage Marrying again after divorce. Also after annulment or widowhood.

sacrament A special action which brings Christians closer to God.

vows Sacred promises a couple make at their marriage.

In pairs, list ten qualities you think make a good relationship between a man and a woman.

For many Christians marriage is a sacrament.

Roles of men and women in a Christian family

ACTIVITIES

What are the roles of the man and the woman in a traditional Christian family?

Some Christian denominations allow women to become ministers.

Traditional roles in a Christian family

Some Christians interpret the second Genesis creation story, which says that God created Adam first, to mean that men are the superior sex. The story tells how Eve was created from Adam's rib bone in order to be his helper. Because Eve was the one who led Adam astray in the Garden of Eden, some Christians believe this teaches that women are the weaker sex.

Some Christians who hold traditional views on marriage believe that the man is the head of a Christian family. In a Christian marriage ceremony the bride would make a vow to obey her husband. Christian women look to Mary, the mother of Jesus, as the role model of a quiet, loving mother. It is the wife's duty to provide a loving home for her husband and children.

They may regard the man as the head of the family with the duty to provide for his wife and children by earning the money. Within the house he sets the rules and leads his family by setting a good example of how a Christian should behave.

These roles are supported by scriptures. St Paul, in his letters to the early Church, gave clear directions that women were to obey their husbands because God had created them that way.

> **Ephesians 5:22–23a**
> *Wives, submit to your husbands as to the Lord. For the husband is the head of the wife as Christ is the head of the Church.*

An alternative view of roles in the Christian family

Most modern Christians do not believe that men are superior to women. This is because in the first creation story it simply says God created human beings to be like himself and that 'male and female he created them' (Genesis 1:27b).

These groups accept that men and women are different, but believe the Bible is saying both are equal in the eyes of God. These views are supported with other passages in the New Testament such as:

> **Galatians 3:28**
>
> *'There is neither... male or female... for you are all one in Christ Jesus.'*
>
> **1 Corinthians 11b–12a**
>
> *'... woman is not independent of man, nor is man independent of woman. For as woman came from man, so also man is born of woman.'*

Most Christians in today's society believe in an equal relationship where the roles of the couple are interchangeable. Some women work to provide for the family and some men share child-care and household duties.

Traditional roles within the Church family

Many Christians think of the members of their religion as one big family, where everyone has a distinct role to play; and they call this the Church family. Following Old Testament passages about the superiority of men, St Paul taught that women should be silent in church.

> **1 Timothy 2:11–13**
>
> *A woman should learn in quietness and full submission. I do not permit a woman to teach or have authority over a man; she must be silent. For Adam was formed first, then Eve.*

Christians suggest that because Jesus chose 12 men to be his disciples, he clearly intended men to take the leading role in the Church. From the disciples Jesus chose Peter to lead the Church and, according to tradition, it was Peter who became the Bishop of Rome, the first Pope. Roman Catholics believe Jesus intended men to be leaders of the Church family and every Pope who has followed Peter has been male. Indeed Roman Catholics do not permit women to become priests.

Other views of the role of men and women in the Church family

Liberal Protestants look at Jesus' treatment of women for guidance. Even though he lived at a time when women had few rights in society, Jesus permitted them to be his followers and showed them respect.

The story of Martha and Mary (Luke 10:38–42) shows Jesus encouraging a woman to sit at his feet in order to learn from him. This was not something women were usually allowed to do.

ACTIVITIES

Write an article for a parish magazine explaining why that particular church believes it is wrong to have a woman priest. Then write a 'letter to the editor' from a female vicar giving the reasons why she thinks that church is wrong.

Christians believe that because the risen Christ chose to reveal himself to women first on Easter morning that it was clear that he held women in high regard.

All this leads less traditional Christians to believe men and women can have an equal role in Church leadership. Most non-conformist Churches permit women to be ministers and the Anglican Church ordained its first women priests in 1994.

Marriage and marriage ceremonies

Marriage ceremonies

Marriage is both a civil and a religious **commitment** for Christians. The Christian **marriage** is a civil ceremony because the couple's relationship is publicly witnessed by the congregation and the marriage register is signed. Christians also believe that marriage is a holy relationship. It is also seen by many Christians as a **sacrament** and part of God's plan for humanity. Through marriage a couple can enjoy a loving relationship with each other that enables God to channel his love for them. Because Christian marriage is a religious commitment, the ceremony takes place in a church or a chapel.

This is how the Catholic Church describes marriage:

> ❝ *Marriage is the sacrament in which baptized men and women vow to belong to each other in a permanent and exclusive sexual partnership of loving, mutual care, concern and shared responsibility, in the hope of having children and bringing up a family.* ❞ *(Catholic Truth Society)*

All Christians believe the purpose of marriage is to:

- help and support each other in good and bad times
- enjoy a sexual relationship
- have children and bring them up in a Christian family.

At a Christian marriage, the ring symbolises that the marriage will be forever.

 **ACTIVITIES**

Make a poster showing the main features of a Christian wedding and their meaning.

What happens in a Christian marriage ceremony?

Although many church weddings are quite lavish affairs, the Christian marriage ceremony is very simple. It requires only the couple, a priest, a ring and two people to witness the ceremony in a church.

The couple will make a promise to each other in the marriage ceremony. It is called a vow because the promise is made in front of God.

> ❝ *I_____, take you _____, to have and to hold, from this day forward: for better, for worse, for richer, for poorer, in sickness and in health, to love and to cherish, till death us do part, according to God's holy law, in the presence of God I make this vow.* ❞

How does the marriage ceremony reflect Christian teachings?

Each part of the marriage ceremony has a meaning which is closely linked to Christian teachings about marriage and family life:

- The ceremony takes place in a church because promises are made in front of God.
- The priest asks the couple and the congregation if there are any reasons why this marriage cannot go ahead. This is to show that the Christian marriage is legally binding.
- The priest asks both the bride and the groom if they want to marry the other person. This is to show that Christian marriage is a relationship, that is entered into freely and no one has forced them to marry.
- Having children and bringing them up in the Christian faith is an important part of marriage and the priest explains this to couples in the opening address.
- Couples say their **vows** in the presence of God and the congregation of Christians as witnesses, showing the sacred importance of the ceremony.
- Prayers, Bible readings and the priest's talk teach the couple about the importance of love in a marriage.
- A ring is given to symbolise the unending nature of love and of Christian marriage. This shows a marriage is for life.

As part of the marriage ceremony, the priest asks the bride and groom 'Will you accept children lovingly from God, and bring them up according to the law of Christ and his Church?'

What do Christians think about civil partnerships?

Christianity teaches that sexual relationships only belong within marriage. For that reason, many Christians do not accept **civil partnerships**. There are several passages in the Bible that condemn same-sex relationships.

> **1 Corinthians 6:9**
> *Do you not know that the wicked will not inherit the kingdom of God? Neither the sexually immoral... nor homosexual offenders.*

The Catholic Church does not accept civil partnerships because it rejects same-sex relationships. In 2008 a Vatican official stated that 'Homosexuality is a disordered behaviour. The activity must be condemned', and the Pope told Catholics that homosexuality was a greater problem for the future of the world than climate change.

Some Christians accept civil partnerships as another form of loving relationship and permit same-sex couples to have a blessing ceremony after their civil partnership registration if they wish. Members of the Church of England vary in their response. Some priests will hold a blessing ceremony after a civil partnership and others will not.

RESEARCH NOTE

Use the BBC news website to research the 2008 case of Lillian Ladele. What reasons did she give for her stand? What did the court decide? Who do you think was right?

AO1 skills ACTIVITIES

Explain why some Christians might say a civil partnership cannot be regarded as a Christian marriage no matter how religious the couple are. What might the couple say?

Divorce

Christian beliefs about the ethics of divorce

Christian teachings and the marriage ceremony, both show Christians that marriage is intended to be a relationship for life. Marriage is a **holy relationship** and the **vows** a couple make are made in front of God and should never be broken. The ring given in the marriage ceremony symbolises that love is unending and that Jesus taught that marriage is for life. These beliefs mean there is much debate within Christianity about whether it is right or wrong to permit married couples to **divorce**.

Roman Catholic beliefs about the ethics of divorce

The reasons discussed above lead Roman Catholics and some Protestants to believe that divorce is wrong. They understand that not all marriages succeed and the Church will give a couple all the assistance it can to help them resolve their differences. When that fails the Catholic Church permits a couple to separate and live apart. It does not allow either of them to re-marry or to have a sexual relationship with anyone else because that would be **adultery**.

In exceptional cases the Catholic Church can officially annul a marriage. This declares that the marriage was not a true marriage and it is cancelled. The situation is the same as if the wedding had never taken place. An **annulment** can be granted if one of the couple was under-age, forced to marry against their will or unaware of what they were doing due to diminished responsibility. An annulment can also be granted if a marriage is not consummated (the couple do not have a sexual relationship after marriage).

The Catholic Catechism says '…men and women… in matrimony give themselves with a love that is total and therefore unique and exclusive' (§2387).

The next two pages will help you to:

- compare beliefs about the ethics of divorce
- examine Christian beliefs about the ethics of re-marriage
- evaluate Christian attitudes about divorce.

HRH Prince Charles and Camilla Parker-Bowles could only have a blessing in church after their marriage because they had both been divorced.

 **ACTIVITIES**

Why was the re-marriage of Prince Charles, heir to the throne and future head of the Church of England, such a difficult issue for the Church of England? The BBC news website may give you some additional information.

Church of England beliefs about the ethics of divorce

Although the Church of England and most Non-conformist Churches believe that marriage is for life, they accept things may not always work out. If this happens the priest will help a couple try to resolve their difficulties. If they are unable to, the Church of England accepts that divorce may be the kindest thing for all concerned because it ends conflict and enables the couple to begin a new life.

- Divorce is permitted because Jesus taught that the right course of action is the most loving thing to do. Forcing a couple to remain trapped in a loveless marriage would hurt them and everyone in their family, which cannot be right.
- Some Christians believe a marriage ends when love dies between the couple, as well as with the death of a partner.
- Others point out that Jesus did allow divorce for unfaithfulness.
- Jesus lived in a Jewish society almost 2000 years ago, so some Christians believe it is right to interpret his message in the light of today's society and permit divorce.

Only the Orthodox Church will grant a religious divorce. Otherwise it is a civil matter that is dealt with through the courts. The 1996 Family Law Act permits divorce for the irretrievable breakdown of a marriage which may have occurred because of adultery, unreasonable behaviour, desertion, two years' separation with consent or five years' separation without consent.

> **Mark 10:10–11**
> *Therefore what God has joined together, let no man separate. Anyone who divorces his wife and marries another woman commits adultery against her.*

> **Matthew 5:32**
> *But I tell you that anyone who divorces his wife, except for marital unfaithfulness, causes her to become an adulteress, and anyone who marries the divorced woman commits adultery.*

Christian beliefs about the ethics of re-marriage

Christians, such as Roman Catholics, do not accept re-marriage in church after a civil divorce. Other Christians accept **re-marriage** because Jesus also taught the importance of forgiveness if someone has made a mistake. However, not all Christians permit a second marriage ceremony to take place in church because the divorced partner would be making promises in front of God which they have already broken once.

The Church of England will accept either re-marriage in church, or a church blessing following a register office ceremony such as the Prince of Wales had. Because some vicars do not believe it is right to make promises which have been broken once, the Church allows them to refuse to carry out a re-marriage ceremony. The couple must marry in another church or with another priest.

AO2 skills **ACTIVITIES**

'My husband and I constantly argue about money. I think we should get divorced but Tim doesn't want to because we have a two-year-old we both love dearly. We are Christians and married in church but I think it's time for each of us to start a fresh life. What should we do?' Write a reply to this magazine letter giving your advice and reasons.

Sexual relationships and contraception

Beliefs about sexual relationships

Christians believe that sex is a gift from God to be enjoyed by a couple as an act of love within their marriage and in order to have children. Because sex is a relationship that has been blessed by God, Christians believe that casual sexual encounters are wrong.

There are many passages in the Bible which teach that sex outside marriage is forbidden. The seventh of the Ten Commandments forbids **adultery**, and some Christians interpret this as meaning that all sexual activity outside marriage is wrong.

Jesus also condemned adultery in the gospels (Mark 10:7–9). This leads some Christians, such as Roman Catholics and Evangelical Protestants, to reject all sexual relationships outside marriage. They believe a person should remain a virgin until they are married and have no other sexual partner during their marriage.

The Catechism of the Catholic Church is very clear about sexual relations: 'The sexual act must take place exclusively within marriage. Outside of marriage it always constitutes a grave sin' (CCC: §2390).

All Christians prefer sexual relationships to take place within a marriage because it provides a stable environment for bringing up children. However, some Christians are prepared to accept pre-marital sex as part of a loving relationship if a couple are committed to each other and plan to marry. This is because Jesus taught that love was what mattered most.

Differing views

Jesus' message of love leads some liberal Christians, such as Quakers, to accept that couples may choose to cohabit (live together without being married) and that some people may choose to enjoy same-sex relationships. These Christians argue that what matters most is the quality of a relationship.

The Church of England, and other Christian groups, believe that marriage is the correct place for a sexual relationship because the family is the best environment to bring up children. They do, however, accept that in today's society many people choose to cohabit as a prelude to getting married. For these reasons **pre-marital sex** may be accepted if marriage is to follow.

> **The next two pages will help you to:**
>
> - examine Christian beliefs about sexual relationships and contraception
> - evaluate views about sexual relationships and contraception.

AO1 skills **ACTIVITIES**

Design an A5 flyer the Catholic Church could give teenagers attending one of their youth clubs, explaining Catholic views about sexual relationships outside marriage.

Adultery is something no Christian would accept because it involves deceit and causes suffering, which can never be right. Not only is it condemned in the Ten Commandments but it breaks the marriage **vows**. Fidelity and commitment are very important aspects of Christian teaching.

> **1 Corinthians 6:18–19a, 20b**
>
> *Flee from sexual immorality. All other sins a man commits are outside his body, but he who sins sexually sins against his own body. Do you not know that your body is a temple of the Holy Spirit … Therefore honour God with your body.*

Beliefs about contraception

Because the marriage ceremony states sex is given to a couple by God so they can have children, Roman Catholics reject the idea of artificial birth control. They believe that the act of sex should always be open to God's gift of a baby. This means the pill, condoms and all other contraceptive devices are forbidden. If a Catholic couple plan a family they are permitted to use a natural method of birth control such as the rhythm method.

Whilst all Christians believe that having children is an important part of marriage, some accept that couples may want to limit the size of their family. This could be for financial reasons or to make sure a woman's health does not suffer as a result of many pregnancies. Provided both husband and wife agree, most forms of contraception are acceptable. This frees a couple to enjoy a sexual relationship without the worry of an unwanted pregnancy. Using contraception to plan the timing of a pregnancy can help ensure that all children in the family are wanted, loved and provided for.

Because the marriage ceremony states that the purpose of marriage is to have children, most Christians do not approve of using contraception to prevent a couple from ever having a baby. For this reason, some Christians do not approve of sterilisation except for medical reasons.

Members of the Christian organisation the 'Silver Ring Thing' promise to abstain from sex before marriage.

 **FOR DEBATE**

'Religion is about spirituality not sexuality.' Should Christians have rules about personal relationships? What do you think?

AO2 skills ACTIVITIES

Explain why some Christians accept contraception and others do not. Summarise Christian beliefs and attitudes about sexual relationships explaining different viewpoints.

Remember and Reflect

The questions in this section are based on the work you have done throughout this Topic. Try to complete as many questions as you can.

The questions in set 1 are designed to test your factual recall and AO1 level skills (knowledge and understanding). The page numbers alongside the questions will help you to find information that might be useful for your answers. Use them to check against what you have written.

The questions in set 2 are more challenging, using AO2 level skills (use of evidence and reasoned argument to evaluate personal responses and differing viewpoints). Your answers many come from more than one part of the Topic.

AO1 Describe, explain and analyse, using knowledge and understanding

Find the answer on:

1 Explain, in one sentence, what each of these words mean:
  a sacrament
  b civil partnership
  c vows
  d annulment
  e adultery
  f promiscuity
  g pre-marital sex
  h commitment
  i divorce
  j re-marriage
	PAGE 96

2 What is the traditional role of a husband in the Christian family?	PAGE 98
3 Give two reasons why a woman should obey her husband in a traditional Christian family.	PAGE 98
4 What does the ring symbolise in a marriage?	PAGE 101
5 Give two reasons why some Christians do not agree with divorce.	PAGE 102, 103
6 Explain why some Christians accept the use of contraception.	PAGE 105
7 State two reasons why some Christians do not agree with sex before marriage.	PAGE 104
8 Describe the Christian wedding ceremony.	PAGE 100, 101
9 What are the three purposes of marriage?	PAGE 100
10 Explain why some Christians accept civil partnerships and others do not.	PAGE 101
11 How is an annulment different from a divorce?	PAGE 102
12 What is the Christian attitude to re-marriage?	PAGE 103
13 Why do some Christians disagree with the use of contraception?	PAGE 105
14 Explain why some Christians believe that men and not women should be Church leaders.	PAGE 99
15 Explain the different Christian attitudes to sex outside marriage.	PAGE 104, 105

AO2 Use evidence and reasoned argument to express and evaluate personal responses, informed insights, and differing viewpoints

1 Do you think everybody should be permitted to celebrate their relationship in church, whether it involves same-sex couples, divorced couples or where one of the couple is an atheist? Why?

2 Draw a spider diagram with *women priests* written in the centre and show the different reasons Christians agree and disagree with this.

3 Some people would say sexual relationships are a matter for the couple themselves. What do you think? Would all Christians agree with you?

4 'Men and women will never have equal roles in a family. It's a biological fact!' Discuss this statement. You should include different, supported points of view and a personal viewpoint. You must refer to Christianity in your answer.

5 Why do you think some Christians will never agree with civil partnerships? Do you think they are right in their view?

6 How would you reply to those who say if Jesus had intended women to be leaders in the church he would have chosen some women disciples?

7 Copy and complete fully the table below explaining different Christian attitudes to:

	Permit it because	Against it because	What my view is
Sex before marriage			
Divorce			
Re-marriage			
Contraception			
Civil partnership			

GradeStudio

Welcome to the Grade Studio

Grade Studio is here to help you improve your answers by working through typical questions you might find on an examination paper. For a full explanation of how this feature works and how exam questions are structured, see page 14. For a full explanation of Assessment Objectives and Levels of Response, see pages x–xi in the Introduction.

AO1 Question

How might a Christian marriage ceremony reflect belief?

[6 marks]

Student's answer

A Christian wedding ceremony reflects belief because the bride wears white, which represents chastity.

People also make vows to each other to say that they will always stay together and look after each other. If someone broke these vows, they might get divorced which is breaking the promise made before God in church.

Comments

The candidate has given a satisfactory answer to the question. There are two relevant points but only one of them, the vows, has any explanation. The answer does not really explain how the service reflects belief, it just states something true about the ceremony. The answer needs to give more information and examples in order to reach Level 3. The candidate could also use more technical terms from the specification to show the breadth of their knowledge and understanding.

Student's improved answer

A Christian wedding ceremony reflects belief in several ways. For example, the bride wears white, which shows that she is still a virgin and is pure.

During the ceremony, which is usually held in a church, the couple also make vows to each other to say that they will stay together for ever and look after each other. If one of the couple breaks these vows they might get divorced.

The major importance of the vows is that they are made before God, so if people break them, they are breaking a promise to God. The ring is also an important part of the service because it symbolises the unity of the two people being married and also the unity of God and God's love which is without end. During the service the priest or minister says that one of the purposes of marriage is for the couple to have children and bring them up as Christians which reflects the beliefs of the couple.

Comments

This is now a good answer to the question. The candidate has shown a sufficiently clear understanding of the question. There is good description and explanation of a variety of different ways in which the service reflects Christian beliefs. The candidate has shown some analysis in dealing with the vows. The information is presented clearly and there is good use of technical terms.

AO2 Question

'Divorce is wrong.' Discuss this statement. You should include different, supported points of view and a personal viewpoint. You must refer to Christianity in your answer.

[12 marks]

Student's answer

Divorce is always wrong for Christians because they promise to stay together until 'death do us part'. Some Christians might also say that if people do get divorced, they are breaking a promise they made to God when they married before a priest as well as to each other. This makes splitting up a really serious matter for Christians and because of this, many of them think divorce is always wrong.

Comments

The candidate has given a limited answer to the question. There are two relevant points but they both address the same issue and neither is expanded very far. In order to reach Level 4, the candidate needs to give alternative viewpoints and to include a personal response.

Student's improved answer

Divorce is always wrong for Christians because they promise to stay together until 'death do us part'.

Some Christians might also say that if people do get divorced, they are breaking a promise they made to God when they married before a priest as well as to each other. This makes splitting up a really serious matter for Christians and because of this, many of them think divorce is always wrong.

On the other hand, some Christians may believe that, if a husband and wife are very unhappy together, they should consider a divorce rather than staying together and being miserable. This can also possibly have a bad effect on their children. Christians will always try to help a couple to stay together, but there are circumstances in which this is not possible. The evidence from the Bible is not clear because Jesus seemed to agree with divorce in the case of adultery. Also a key idea in Christianity is forgiveness and some Christians believe divorced people, need to be forgiven so they can move on into a new relationship rather than be miserable for ever. I think divorce should be allowed.

My personal opinion is that sometimes people are just not suited to one another and that they are better off getting a divorce and having the opportunity to start their life again. However, I do think that it is important that the needs of any children are taken into account when a divorce takes place.

Comments

This is now a good answer to the question. The candidate has shown a clear understanding of the question and has presented a range of views supported by evidence and argument. The answer explains Christian views, amongst others, and includes a personal viewpoint, which is also supported.

These specimen answers provide an outline of how you could construct your response. Space does not allow us to give a full response. You will need to provide more detail in your actual exam responses.

Topic 8: Religion and medical ethics

The Big Picture

In this Topic, you will be addressing Christian beliefs about:

- abortion and the reasons for different attitudes to this issue
- fertility treatment and attitudes to issues raised by fertility treatment and cloning
- euthanasia and suicide and the reasons for different attitudes to these issues
- the use of animals in medical research.

You will also think about your own feelings and responses to these questions and issues.

DID YOU KNOW?

- Every year at least 200,000 women have abortions in the UK.
- Some Christians believe abortion is the greatest moral evil.
- When anaesthetics were discovered in the 19th century some Christians accused doctors of 'playing God'.
- It is theoretically possible to choose the sex of a baby, perhaps for the reason of preventing the transmission of diseases which are carried by one gender; for example, muscular dystrophy affects only boys.

KEY WORDS

abortion Deliberate termination of pregnancy by removal and destruction of the foetus.

clone An individual organism or cell produced asexually from one ancestor to which they are genetically identical.

embryo A foetus before it is 4 months old.

euthanasia When someone is helped to die without pain before they would have died naturally.

fertility treatment Medical treatment to help a woman become pregnant.

genetic engineering The deliberate modification of the characteristics of an organism by manipulating its genetic material.

medical ethics Questions of morality that are raised by medical situations.

sacred/sanctity Holy, having something of God or the divine.

sanctity of life The belief that all life is given by God and is therefore sacred.

suicide Deliberately ending one's own life.

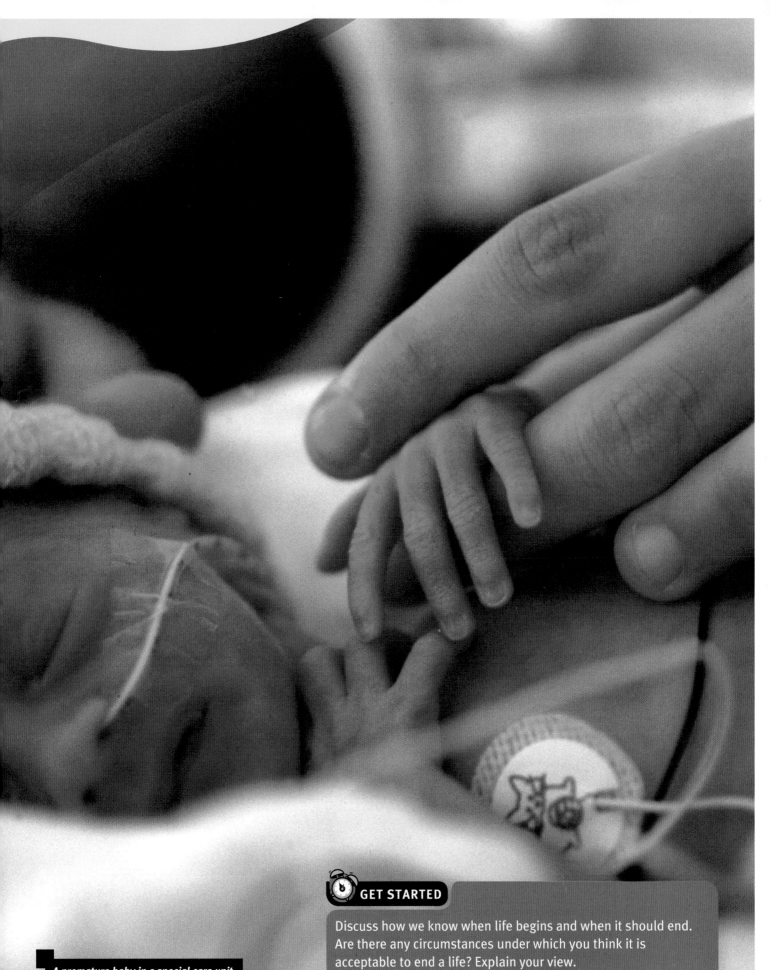

A premature baby in a special care unit.

GET STARTED

Discuss how we know when life begins and when it should end. Are there any circumstances under which you think it is acceptable to end a life? Explain your view.

Attitudes to abortion

What is medical ethics?

Medical ethics is about applying moral values to medical situations. The following questions are examples of the kind of dilemmas which medical ethics deals with:

- Should everyone have the right to have a child, helped by doctors if necessary?
- Should people be kept alive if they are very disabled or in great pain?
- Should women be able to end a pregnancy if they choose?

Is life sacred?

Many Christians have strong views about medical ethics because they believe that life is created by God. It is therefore **sacred** or holy and humans do not have the right to take it away. This is often described as the '**sanctity of life**' and is a concept used in arguments about whether particular actions are right or wrong. Knowing when a human life begins is very important for Christians in helping them to decide if and when abortion is acceptable.

When does human life begin?

Today many pregnant women have their first ultrasound scan at 8 weeks and are able to see, even at such an early stage, that their baby is beginning to be recognisably human.

Some doctors say that, although the technology used to produce pictures like this is fantastic, such images confuse people. Donald Peebles, a scientist at University College Hospital, London said in a newspaper interview that although the foetus clearly looks human by 12 weeks, proper sensory development takes place much later. He believed that there was risk that the pictures would make people assume that foetuses have more advanced brains than is the case (*The Times*, 3 October 2006).

The next two pages will help you to:

- explain and evaluate Christian beliefs about the sanctity of life
- evaluate the reasons for different attitudes to abortion
- reflect on your own views about these issues.

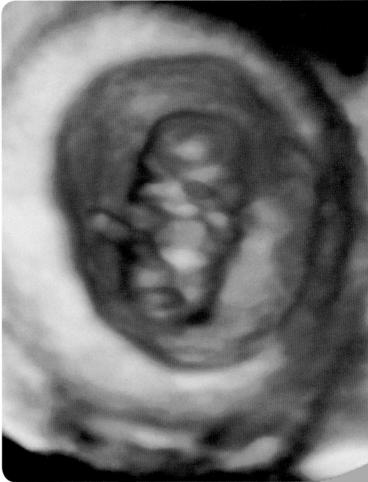

A 3D scan of a four-week-old foetus.

AO1 skills ACTIVITIES

With a partner write a sentence of not more than ten words explaining the meaning of the term 'sanctity of life'. Compare your sentence with others in the group.

What is abortion?

Abortion is the deliberate termination of pregnancy by the removal and destruction of the foetus. Each year in the UK more than 200,000 women have abortions. Around 4000 of those are on girls aged under 16, the legal age of consent for sex. In the UK abortions are legal if the foetus is less than 24 weeks old, provided two doctors consent to the abortion. It has to be done before the baby could live outside the womb without medical help.

Abortions over 24 weeks are only allowed in exceptional circumstances, for example, if there is a substantial risk that the child would be born with a serious disability, if the mother's life is in danger or if a woman has become pregnant as a result of rape.

Why do Christians disagree about abortion?

There is no specific teaching in the Bible about abortion so Christians have to apply their understanding of Christian principles to the situation. Different ways of interpreting the teachings in the Bible result in Christians having different attitudes to abortion.

Many Christians believe that all babies have a soul from the moment of conception and so are fully human. This is based on the teaching in Genesis 1:27 that people are made in the image of God; that God has a plan for every individual (Jeremiah 1:5) and that God is the creative spark from the moment of conception (Psalm 139:13). This means that they believe the foetus is fully human and therefore abortion is the same as murder.

Both the Church of England and the Roman Catholic Church teach that abortion is a great moral evil and that human life must be protected and respected from the moment of conception.

The Roman Catholic Church does not permit abortion under any circumstances unless it is the unintended but foreseeable result of an action, i.e. 'doctrine of double effect'. For example, when an operation necessary to save the life of the mother causes the abortion, such as in an ectopic pregnancy.

The Church of England teaches that abortion is only acceptable in exceptional circumstances, for example, if it is necessary to save the mother's life, if the pregnancy is the result of rape, or if the baby is likely to be severely disabled. Other Christians take a broader view but believe abortion should be a last resort, and the parents must make the final decision.

Genesis 1:27

So God created man in his own image, in the image of God he created him; male and female he created them.

Jeremiah 1:5a

Before I formed you in the womb I knew you, before you were born I set you apart.

RESEARCH NOTE

At 4–6 weeks the foetus is the size of a poppy seed; its heart is a single tube with a few uncoordinated beats; bones begin to form. Find out about the development of a foetus/embryo at 8, 12, 20, 28 and 40 weeks. How can this information be used in the arguments for and against abortion?

AO2 skills ACTIVITIES

'One question about all this is: why is it when I wanted the baby it was a baby, and when I didn't it was something else?' (Ellie, aged 20, in online chat room about abortion). How would you respond to Ellie's question? Explain your reasons.

What do Christians believe about fertility treatment?

The ethics of fertility treatment

Fertility treatment, cloning and **genetic engineering** raise some important ethical questions for many Christians. Three important beliefs affect the way Christians view these issues:

- God alone should be the creator of life.
- God gave humans a soul.
- God created humans in his image.

What is fertility treatment?

Fertility treatment is medical treatment given to help people who want babies but cannot have them. The reasons for infertility can be that the man is not producing healthy sperm or the woman is not producing eggs. Whatever the reason, infertility can make people very unhappy.

Christian responses to issues raised by fertility treatment

Christians do not agree about fertility treatment. Roman Catholics disagree with fertility treatment and teach that infertility must be accepted as part of God's plan. Many Christians think that medical help should be given to people who want babies. Some Christians think it is wrong to use sperm or eggs from a donor because it brings a third person into the marriage relationship.

In vitro fertilisation (IVF)

One of the most common fertility treatments is IVF, which stands for *In vitro* fertilisation – literally meaning 'in glass'. Doctors put healthy sperm and a human egg together in a test tube and wait to see if embryos develop. Embryos are then placed inside a woman's uterus where they can continue to grow. To ensure that at least one embryo survives doctors fertilise more than one egg. This process may result in spare embryos. Many Christians and non-religious people are concerned about what happens to these spare embryos.

Using donor sperm or eggs

Sometimes one partner cannot produce healthy sperm or eggs at all and donor sperm or eggs may be used. There are questions about whether it is acceptable to use donor sperm or eggs from someone who is unknown to the couple. Some Christians think this goes against the belief that partners should be faithful to each other.

The next two pages will help you to:

- explain and evaluate Christian responses to issues raised by fertility treatment and cloning
- reflect on your own views about these issues.

 **ACTIVITIES**

With a partner think of as many reasons as you can why people might want to have children.

 **ACTIVITIES**

Do spare embryos count as potential humans and would it be committing murder to throw them away if they are not needed?

Is it right to use embryos for medical research?

Christians believe in the **sanctity of life**. They believe life is a gift from God and trust that God has a purpose for each human life. The ability of scientists to use human embryos to **clone** human cells raises significant ethical problems for many Christians. Some Christians who are opposed to human cloning see it as morally equivalent to 'playing God'.

In embryo research human embryos are studied and used in order to find ways of preventing and curing illnesses. Human tissue from the embryos can be implanted into living patients to slow down serious diseases of the nervous system such as motor neurone disease and Parkinson's disease. This tissue usually comes from aborted foetuses.

Roman Catholics oppose all embryo research. Anglicans support it up to 14 days. Most Christians accept controlled embryo research. Some Christians think that embryo research is acceptable because it means that some good comes out of **abortions**. Others disagree because they think it is treating human life as a means to an end rather than as intrinsically valuable, and because the embryo is not in a position to give consent.

Is cloning playing God?

In 1996 the world's first cloned animal, Dolly the sheep, was created by cell fusion in which the nucleus of an already differentiated adult cell was fused with an unfertilised egg from a donor animal. It is theoretically possible to use this process to produce a child that is a clone, an exact image, of one of its parents.

Playing God: Frankenstein's Monster

In 1818 Mary Shelley's book *Frankenstein* was published. This tells the story of scientist Victor Frankenstein and the monster he created from parts of dead bodies with disastrous consequences. It seemed a total fantasy when it was written but, 200 years later, at the start of the 21st century, it no longer seems impossible.

Are we 'Playing God' by choosing the kind of baby we want?

She may never get breast cancer – but girl's birth raises new doubts over designer babies

In 2009 scientists announced that they had screened embryos for the purpose of reducing a baby's chance of getting breast cancer when she grows up. This was not a case of a so-called 'designer baby' – her parents did not choose her hair colour or select an aptitude for maths or ice skating. They did it to ensure that she did not develop a life threatening disease and that she would not pass on the defective gene to her own children.

RESEARCH NOTE

'Religion should not interfere with how people conceive.'

Research on the Internet arguments for and against this statement.

Frankenstein's monster as depicted in the film Frankenstein *(1931).*

AO2 skills **ACTIVITIES**

What arguments could be put forward to support the claim that a person created by cloning was 'made in the image of God'? Do you agree?

Attitudes to euthanasia and suicide

Should we have the right to choose when we die?

Most Christians believe that God gives life and only God can decide when a life should be ended. Some Christians believe that as humans have free will they have a choice between life and death but to choose death, either by **euthanasia** or **suicide**, would be a sin.

ACTIVITIES

Discuss with a partner how you might support a friend who was feeling very depressed.

> **Job 1:21b**
> *The Lord gave and the Lord has taken away, may the name of the Lord be praised.*

Euthanasia, sometimes called 'mercy killing', means 'good or gentle death' and is used to describe situations where death is deliberately chosen either by the person or by people close to them if they are unable to make the choice themselves.

It is against the law in the UK but legal elsewhere, for example in the Netherlands and Switzerland. It can be voluntary, known as 'assisted suicide', or 'involuntary', which is when other people decide someone's life should end. However, withdrawal of treatment is not illegal in the UK and if the patient requests this then treatment must be stopped. This is called 'passive euthanasia'.

'Active euthanasia' is when deliberate action is taken to end life, using a lethal injection or administering a fatal dose of a drug. Many Christians would not differentiate between these ways of ending life arguing that, however good the motive, it is still killing. Christians often work to care for people who are dying by supporting the hospice movement.

RESEARCH NOTE

Find out about the work of Dame Cicely Saunders who founded the hospice movement.

The case of Dan James

In December 2008 23-year-old Dan James, who had broken his neck in a rugby accident in March 2007, ended his life, supported by his family, and helped by Dignitas, a Swiss clinic specialising in assisted suicide.

In an email to *Times Online* his mother, Julie, explains her decision to help Dan kill himself.

> *Three weeks ago our son was at last allowed his wish of a dignified death in the Dignitas apartment in Zurich. Dan was 23 years old and had broken his neck in a rugby accident in March 2007. He couldn't walk, had no hand function, but constant pain in all of his fingers. He was incontinent, suffered uncontrollable spasms in his legs and upper body and needed 24-hour care. Dan had tried to commit suicide three times but this was unsuccessful due to his disability. His only other option was to starve himself. Dan had been a lively and hugely active young man he was highly intelligent, lovable and so loved by his family. Whilst not everyone in Dan's situation would find it as unbearable as Dan, what right does any human being have to tell any other that they have to live such a life, filled with terror, discomfort and indignity, what right does one person who chooses to live with a particular illness or disability have to tell another that they should have to. ... Nobody but nobody should judge him or anyone else.*

Suicide

Suicide is when someone ends their own life. It is sometimes called 'self-murder' and was once treated as a crime. A person who tried to take their own life but failed could receive the death penalty. Roman Catholics believe it is a sin which would exclude someone from heaven. For a long time people who committed suicide were not allowed to be buried in the consecrated ground of churchyards. Today, although most Christians think it is morally wrong, their view has moved from being judgemental to being compassionate. People have a better understanding of the reasons why someone may want to end their own life, because they are very depressed, for example.

The Samaritans is an organisation set up in 1953 by Rev. Chad Varah, a Christian vicar, in the crypt of his London church, to provide 24-hour telephone counselling for people who feel suicidal and need someone to talk to. He started the Samaritans to 'befriend the suicidal and despairing', after conducting the funeral of a 13-year-old girl who had killed herself.

This is how his son Michael described their work: 'They give the sad person their total attention. They completely forget themselves. They listen... and listen... and listen without interrupting. We call them "Samaritans"'. Chad Varah died in 2007 but the Samaritan volunteers still provide a 24-hour service via phone, email, letter and face to face.

Dan James (1985–2008).

 **ACTIVITIES**

Sometimes a moral choice may be between two opposing goods rather than simply between right and wrong. This may be the case when someone is deciding whether to help another person end their life because it has become intolerable – what do you think?

Do animals have rights?

An artist's impression of the laboratory mouse grown by Dr Vacanti in 1995. The experiment was intended to show how replacement tissues can be grown to replace damaged human tissue.

Christian beliefs about the relationship between humans and animals

Christians believe that humans are made in the image of God. They are the most important part of creation and God gave them control over all other living things. This is based on Genesis 1:26 which describes how God gave humans power over all other living things. Most Christians believe that animals do not have souls and so cannot have the same relationship with God as humans. Therefore, some people believe that their lives have less importance than those of humans.

Most Christians see their role in relation to the natural world not as that of 'rulers' to control and exploit it but as stewards with a responsibility to care for and respect God's creation.

Jesus taught that God cares about the smallest creatures and that not one sparrow will fall to the ground without God knowing about it. He stressed that humans are worth more than sparrows and that God knows every hair on their heads (Matthew 10:29–30). Christians believe they should try to follow the example of a loving God, showing care and compassion.

ACTIVITIES

Work with a partner to create a mind map showing ways humans use animals. Use different colours to indicate uses which may exploit animals and those which promote a good relationship. Share your maps with the class.

RESEARCH NOTE

Research and prepare a short presentation about the lives of St Francis of Assisi and St Philip Neri and their treatment of animals.

> **Genesis 1:26a, 28**
>
> *Then God said, 'Let us make man in our image, in our likeness… God blessed them and said to them, "Be fruitful and increase in number; fill the earth and subdue it. Rule over the fish of the sea and the birds of the air and over every living thing that moves on the ground."'*

Christian beliefs about the use of animals in experiments

Although many Christians believe that animals do not have souls and are not aware of their existence in the same way as humans, they do not think it is acceptable to be cruel to animals. This would be a failure of their responsibility as stewards of God's creation. They would be showing a lack of respect for creation and, therefore, for God.

Christians recognise that humans can benefit from experiments on animals. For example, animal experiments led directly to the development of dialysis machines to treat kidney failure and to the development of drugs to prevent rejection in organ transplants. Such experiments were also central in creating vaccines for tuberculosis, which kills 3 million people every year.

Therefore, most Christians believe that it is acceptable to use animals for medical research if it is essential for the good of humans. However they stress that unnecessary suffering must be avoided, as causing pain to animals would not be compatible with living according to the teachings of Jesus. Most Christians would argue that if animal testing could result in a cure for a serious disease then it would be acceptable, provided as little suffering as possible was caused to the animal.

In 1995 Dr J. Vacanti, a transplant surgeon, grew what appeared to be a human ear onto the back of a mouse. When photos emerged the following year, they caused outrage among members of the animal rights and pro-life groups who thought the mouse had been genetically engineered. In reality, the growth originated from cow cartilage (no human tissue was used) that was transplanted into the mouse, and was not the result of genetic engineering. Dr Vacanti said that the same technique might make it possible to grow a liver, saving the lives of people who die waiting for a liver transplant.

How far should we go?

The possibility of genetically modifying the bodies of animals so that they can be used to grow spare parts for humans also means that it is possible for scientists to create hybrid creatures. Patents for such developments have already been filed in the USA. What are the problems of such developments? What rights would they have?

REMEMBER THIS

Look back at the issues raised by the story of Frankenstein's monster in 8.2 to help you think about whether it is acceptable to use genetic engineering to create creatures for experiments.

ACTIVITIES

Is it natural for scientists to want to keep pushing the boundaries of what is possible? If so, what checks must be made to ensure that what is done is ethically acceptable? Just because we *can* do something, does that mean we *should*? *Who* decides and *how* do we decide?

Remember and Reflect

The questions in this section are based on the work you have done throughout this Topic. Try to complete as many questions as you can.

The questions in set 1 are designed to test your factual recall and AO1 level skills (knowledge and understanding). The page numbers alongside the questions will help you to find information that might be useful for your answers. Use them to check against what you have written.

The questions in set 2 are more challenging, using AO2 level skills (use of evidence and reasoned argument to evaluate personal responses and differing viewpoints). Your answers many come from more than one part of the Topic.

AO1 Describe, explain and analyse, using knowledge and understanding

Find the answer on:

1 Explain what each of the following key words means. Use one sentence for each word.
   a abortion
   b euthanasia
   c cloning
   d sanctity of life
   e medical ethics
   f suicide

PAGE 110

2 Give three examples of questions which focus on medical ethics.

PAGE 112

3 Give three legal reasons why a woman may have an abortion.

PAGE 113

4 Explain the Roman Catholic view on abortion and the reasons for it.

PAGE 113

5 Give two references to teachings in the Bible that a Christian might use to argue against abortion.

PAGE 113

6 Give two examples of fertility treatments and explain Christian views about whether they are acceptable or not.

PAGE 114

7 What is a 'spare embryo' and what problems does the use of spare embryos in medical research raise for Christians?

PAGE 114

8 Why do the issues raised by genetic engineering remind some people of the story of Frankenstein's monster?

PAGE 115

9 Why is euthanasia sometimes called 'mercy killing'?

PAGE 116

10 Explain why Christians might have different opinions about euthanasia.

PAGE 116, 117

11 'The Lord gave and the Lord has taken away, may the name of the Lord be praised' (Job 1:21b). Why are these words often used at Christian funerals? How do they support the view of some Christians that euthanasia and suicide are wrong?

PAGE 116, 117

12 Give an example of how Christians might try to support and care for people who are dying.

PAGE 116

13 What do Christians believe about the relationship between humans and animals? Explain how they justify their view by referring to teaching, from the Bible.

PAGE 118

14 Give two examples of how experiments on animals have led to life-saving treatments for humans.

PAGE 119

AO2 Use evidence and reasoned argument to express and evaluate personal responses, informed insights, and differing viewpoints

1   Why do you think the beginning and end of life poses so many difficult questions for religious people, philosophers and people with no religious beliefs?

2   'Abortion is murder!' How would you respond to someone who holds this view? Explain the reasons for your response.

3   Do you think that women who claim that they have the right to treat their body however they choose should include the need to treat it responsibly by preventing the risk of unwanted pregnancy? Explain your reasons.

4   'Humans should always protect and preserve life and never destroy it.' Do you agree or disagree? Explain your reasons.

5   'Embryo research is so important in finding treatments for some terrible illnesses Christians should encourage it.' Do you agree? Give reasons to support your answer and show you have thought about different points of view.

6   Is the argument 'We should because we can' an acceptable argument for supporting cloning and other aspects of genetic engineering? Give clear reasons to support your view.

7   'Animals do not have rights but humans have a moral responsibility to treat them properly.' Discuss this statement referring to Christian beliefs and your own views, giving reasons for them.

8   Think back over the issues you have studied in this Topic. What do you think is the most difficult question for medical ethics and why?

GradeStudio

Welcome to the Grade Studio

Grade Studio is here to help you improve your answers by working through typical questions you might find on an examination paper. For a full explanation of how this feature works and how exam questions are structured, see page 14. For a full explanation of Assessment Objectives and Levels of Response, see pages x–xi in the Introduction.

AO1 Question

Explain Christian attitudes to the use of animals in medical research.   **[6 marks]**

Student's answer

Christians believe that God placed humans in charge of the world and in charge of the animals.

Some Christians believe that, because humanity was placed in charge of the animals, we can eat them and do anything else that we wish with them. Their life is not as valuable as human life, so if animals can help save human lives, this is a good reason to conduct medical research on them.

Comments

The candidate has given a satisfactory answer to the question. There are two relevant points, but they are not explained in any detail. In order to reach Level 3, the answer needs to give more information and examples. The candidate could also use more technical terms from the specification to show the breadth of their knowledge and understanding.

Student's improved answer

Christians believe that God placed humans in charge of the world and in charge of the animals. Some Christians believe that, because humanity was placed in charge of the animals, we can eat them and do anything else that we wish with them. Their life is not as valuable as human life, so if animals can help save human lives, this is a good reason to conduct medical research on them.

Some Christians might say that this is using animals as a type of lesser creation, and that there is no basis for this. In fact, God placed a responsibility on people to look after creation known as stewardship and misusing animals goes against this. Many Christians are also concerned as to what experiments take place on animals. While some people may be reasonably happy with experiments on animals that lead to cures for human diseases, especially if there is no other way of carrying out the research, they may be much less happy with experiments to test cosmetics or other tests which are not necessary and are simply taking place for human convenience. Many Christians believe that the responsible thing to do is to try to find ways of researching cures for disease using as few animals as possible.

Comments

This is now a good answer to the question. The candidate has shown a clear understanding of the question. There is good description and explanation of a variety of different responses that Christians might have in relation to animals. The candidate has shown good analysis in dealing with the question of experiments on animals. The information is presented clearly and there is good use of technical terms.

AO2 Question

'Every woman has the right to have a baby.' Discuss this statement. You should include different, supported points of view and a personal viewpoint. You must refer to Christianity in your answer. **[12 marks]**

Student's answer

Christians might say that women are designed by God to have babies and that therefore every woman has the right to have one. Some Christians might also say that, if a woman is not able to have a baby by natural means, she should be able to have fertility treatment because God has enabled scientists to discover this. God tells people in the Old Testament to multiply so every woman has a right to if they are able.

Comments

The candidate has given a limited answer to the question. There are two relevant points but neither is expanded very far. In order to reach Level 4 the answer needs to give alternative viewpoints and to include a personal response.

Student's improved answer

Christians might say that women are designed by God to have babies and that therefore every woman has the right to have one. Some Christians might also say that, if a woman is not able to have a baby by natural means, she should be able to have fertility treatment because God has enabled scientists to discover this. God tells people in the Old Testament to multiply, so every woman has a right to if they are able.

Other Christians might say that a baby is a gift, not a right, and that if God wanted a woman to have a baby then she would have one. The fact that she cannot conceive naturally means that she was not intended to have a baby. God has other plans for her rather than being a mother. Others may say that this sort of statement means that single mothers and lesbians would also have the right to have babies, and they would not approve of this because the baby will not be brought up in a traditional family unit. I find it difficult to decide about this issue.

My personal opinion is that there is no simple answer to this question. I do understand that many women are desperate to have a baby and may not be able to have one naturally, so they will want fertility treatment. However, it is also true that there are a lot of questions to be answered about single women choosing to have a baby without a father.

Comments

This is now a good answer to the question. The candidate has shown a clear understanding of the question and has presented a range of views supported by evidence and argument. The answer explains Christian views, amongst others, and includes a personal viewpoint, which is also supported.

These specimen answers provide an outline of how you could construct your response. Space does not allow us to give a full response. You will need to provide more detail in your actual exam responses.

Topic 9: Religion, poverty and wealth

The Big Picture

In this Topic, you will be addressing religious beliefs and teachings about:

- Christian views of wealth and the causes of hunger, poverty and disease
- what the Bible says about concern for others, and different ways in which Christians might put charity into practice
- Christian teachings about the use of money, and donating to charity
- Christian teachings about moral and immoral occupations and the impact these teachings have on believers.

You will also think about the ways in which these beliefs affect the life and outlook of Christians in today's world.

DID YOU KNOW?

- According to the charity Shelter 3.8 million children in the UK live in poverty once their housing costs have been paid.
- According to the UN 25,000 people die every day of hunger or hunger-related causes, despite there being enough food in the world to feed everyone.
- The charity Christian Aid gave more than £66 million in aid to more than 50 countries, including the UK.
- Christian charities such as CAFOD and Christian Aid help people of any religion and those who do not follow a religion.

KEY WORDS

charity To give help or money to those in need.

compassion Sympathy and concern for others.

ecumenical Different Christian denominations working together.

immoral Not conforming to accepted standards of behaviour.

LEDC Less economically developed country.

MEDC More economically developed country.

moral Conforming to accepted standards of behaviour.

philanthropist Someone who donates money, goods, services or time to help a cause which benefits society.

tithe The Christian practice of giving a tenth of their income to charity.

trade restrictions Restrictions made by one country about the amounts and types of goods it will allow into the country from other countries.

In 1984, 1989 and 2004 many famous singers came together to perform concerts and record songs to raise awareness of poverty in African countries. What are the advantages and disadvantages of such large and irregular campaigns?

Christian beliefs about the causes of hunger, poverty and disease

What does Christianity say about the causes of hunger, poverty and disease?

Hunger

Many **more economically developed countries** (MEDCs) have **trade restrictions**, or taxes, which prevent **less economically developed countries** (LEDCs) from selling high-value processed goods to them. This means that, for example, an LEDC can sell raw coffee beans to an MEDC at a low price. The coffee beans are then processed into instant coffee by a manufacturer from the MEDC and sold on for a much higher price. However if the LEDC tried to process and sell instant coffee the **trade restrictions**, or taxes, would mean they were unable to make even a small profit.

Many large companies based in MEDCs set up factories in LEDCs, where wages are much lower, to maximise their profits. In some of these factories the working conditions are so poor that they would not be allowed to operate in the UK.

Many Christians feel it is unfair for MEDCs to prevent LEDCs from developing a more profitable economy, or to exploit their workers. Traidcraft is a Christian organisation which aims to bring about fairer trade practices, and reduce poverty by supplying fair trade products to the UK.

Some Christians may believe that hunger in the world is largely brought about by the greed of certain countries at the expense of others. They may also refer to teachings such as the parable of The Sheep and the Goats (Matthew 25:31–46) as an example of how Christians should treat people less fortunate than themselves.

The next two pages will help you to:

- explain Christian beliefs about the causes of hunger, poverty and disease
- reflect on your own responses to these issues.

AO1 skills ACTIVITIES

Working in pairs, consider why some people are very poor and some are very rich. Make a list of possible reasons then share them with the class.

A child in a slum city in India.

RESEARCH NOTE

Visit the Traidcraft website and find out how buying fair trade products helps people in LEDCs.

Poverty

In the past MEDCs encouraged LEDCs to borrow money from them. The interest rates then increased, and the LEDCs have sometimes been unable to repay the loan. In some cases the original amount of the loan has been paid back many times over, but as the interest is added then the loans are still not paid off.

Some Christians might feel that the practices used in loaning money to LEDCs amount to usury. Usury can mean loaning money at any interest rate, but is usually interpreted by Christians today as charging interest at an unfairly high rate. Usury is forbidden in the Old Testament, and the Prophet Ezekiel considered it as bad as robbery.

Although many Christians do borrow and lend money they still believe that this should not be done at the expense of the poor. The gospels are full of examples and teachings about caring for the poor and this is a central part of Christian belief and practice.

> **Ezekiel 18:8–9**
> *He does not lend at usury or take excessive interest.*

Natural disasters

Many parts of the world are subject to natural disasters, such as floods, droughts, hurricanes and volcanic eruptions. In LEDCs such events are more likely to lead to death because these countries cannot afford to take the same kind of preventative measures as MEDCs, and do not have access to the same kind of emergency services.

In the past some Christians tended to see natural disasters as punishments for not being faithful to God. Today some still see natural disasters as being performed by the Devil. They might believe the Devil is trying to make people feel God is not helping them, to destroy their faith.

However, many Christians might point to the role humans play in natural disasters. For example, heavy rain may cause flooding where forests have been cut down to make quick profits. These Christians might then point to the selfishness of those who make a profit for themselves without thinking about the impact of their actions on the world as a whole.

Disease

In some countries children are more likely to die of diseases such as measles because there is no vaccination programme. In other countries, lack of access to clean drinking water means people die of diseases such as cholera. The World Health Organisation (WHO) in 2003 estimated that of the 6 million people with HIV/AIDS in LEDCs, only 300,000 were actually receiving treatment.

Some Christians feel that the poverty which prevents people accessing healthcare is unacceptable, and call for drug companies to make their products available more cheaply in poorer countries.

As with poverty most Christians would see the causes of disease as being the result of the exploitation of the poor. However, in the time of the New Testament it was believed that some illnesses were the result of sin. When Jesus healed a blind man he said: 'Receive your sight; your faith has healed you' (Luke 18:42b).

FOR DEBATE

Some baby products have recently offered to donate the cost of a tetanus vaccination (approximately 86p) to a well-known charity for every specially marked product sold. Is this a good way to help LEDCs?

AO2 skills ACTIVITIES

Create a mind map showing all the factors which contribute to hunger, poverty and disease. Highlight those causes which could be changed by individual action in one colour, and those which need changes by governments and organisations in another. How might a Christian try to respond to these issues?

Religious views of poverty and wealth

The next two pages will help you to:

- explain Christian attitudes to wealth and the use of money
- explain Christian responses to poverty
- identify and reflect on your own views about issues to do with wealth and poverty.

Christian attitudes to wealth and poverty

Many Christians do not see a problem with being wealthy, but they do believe that wealth should be used appropriately. However, they also believe that it is part of the Christian duty to help people who are less fortunate than themselves.

Some Christians see wealth as a temptation which leads some people to behave in a less Christian manner, so they believe that wealth needs to be handled with care. If wealth is used in an appropriate manner then heaven will still be accessible.

What does the Bible say about wealth and poverty?

Throughout the Bible there are teachings about wealth and poverty in both the Old and New Testaments. People are encouraged to look after the poor:

> **Deuteronomy 15:11**
> *There will always be poor people in the land. Therefore I command you to be open handed toward your brothers and toward the poor and needy in your land.*

This is seen as a form of worship:

> **Proverbs 14:31**
> *He who oppresses the poor shows contempt for their Maker, but whoever is kind to the needy honours God.*

People are also warned of the dangers of loving money as it can interfere with loving God:

> **Matthew 6:24**
> *No one can serve two masters. Either he will hate the one and love the other, or he will be devoted to the one and despise the other. You cannot serve both God and Money.*

> **Matthew 19:24**
> *Again I tell you it is easier for a camel to go through the eye of a needle than for a rich man to enter the kingdom of God.*

 **ACTIVITIES**

Look carefully at the Bible quotes on this page. What attitudes to wealth and poverty do they show? How might these views affect the ways in which Christians see wealth and poverty today?

FOR DEBATE

Do you think being wealthy makes it harder to be good?

Jesus answered:

> **Matthew 19:21**
> *If you want to be perfect, go, sell your possessions and give to the poor, and you will have treasure in heaven. Then come, follow me.*

Finally, people are warned that they must acquire money honestly:

> **Proverbs 13:11**
> *Dishonest money dwindles away but he who gathers money little by little makes it grow.*

The Bristol City Museum and Art Gallery.

How have some Christians used their wealth?

In Edinburgh in the 1800s the Nelsons (a Christian family), who made their money from printing and publishing, built four libraries for the use of working men, and contributed to the building of the Royal Infirmary.

In the second half of the 19th century, in the UK, Thomas Barnardo, with the financial support of other Christian **philanthropists**, such as Lord Shaftesbury, set up a series of homes to help destitute children. The organisation he founded still exists today helping children and their families.

In the 1800s and 1900s the Wills family in Bristol, who had made their fortune in tobacco, made generous donations to Bristol University and to the City's Museum and Art Gallery.

In November 2008 Christian philanthropists offered £90,000 to support five Christian charities following a 'Dragons' Den' style presentation.

What do the Churches say about wealth today?

Christian Action on Poverty (CAP) is an **ecumenical** group set up to address the issues of poverty in the UK. In the past they have encouraged Christians to live on the minimum wage during the 40 days of Lent, to develop their understanding of poverty, and to donate any money they have saved to organisations which reduce poverty.

In 2006 Pope Benedict XVI argued that LEDCs should be allowed to trade more fairly with MEDCs so that they could generate more wealth and reduce poverty. In 2008 the Bishop of Rochester, the Right Reverend Dr Nazir-Ali, argued that high earners should be sharing their wealth with others rather than simply trying to make more money for themselves.

REMEMBER THIS

Ecumenical refers to a situation where people from churches of different denominations work together.

 **ACTIVITIES**

Do you think Christian teachings on wealth and poverty are fair?

How do you feel about the fact that some people have so much money when others are dying through lack of food or clean water?

Concern for others

The Salvation Army work to help the poor and homeless.

What are the Christian teachings about caring for those in need?

The Bible is quite clear that Christians have a duty to support the poor. Look at the teachings below and consider how they might be put into practice.

These teachings are found in the Old Testament as well as the New Testament. The first text shows that people who do not care for the poor will suffer themselves:

> **Proverbs 21:13**
>
> *If a man shuts his ears to the cry of the poor, he too will cry out and not be answered.*

> **1 John 3:17–18**
>
> *If anyone has material possessions and sees his brother in need but has no pity on him, how can the love of God be in him? Dear children, let us not love with words or tongue but with actions and in truth.*

Christians are told that they should give money privately and not advertise their generosity:

> **Matthew 6:2**
>
> *So when you give to the needy, do not announce it with trumpets, as the hypocrites do in the synagogues and on the streets, to be honoured by men. I tell you the truth, they have received their reward in full.*

These teachings clearly show that Christians should help the poor and show **compassion**. However, they should do so discreetly, and not in such a way as to attract undue attention to their deeds. It is the fact that they have helped the poor which is important, not that they receive recognition for doing so.

> **Mark 12:42–43**
>
> *But a poor widow came and put in two very small copper coins, worth only a fraction of a penny.*
> *Calling his disciples to him, Jesus said, 'I tell you the truth, this poor widow has put more into the treasury than all the others.'*

This final passage shows that the size of what is given is not important. It is the intention and cost to the giver which is more significant.

How do Christians put these teachings into practice?

In the Old Testament a tenth (or **tithe**) of the harvest was given to God's work. Some Christians today still donate a percentage of their income to **charity**. They might donate this money to their church, or give it to charity. Some Christians donate this money to a Christian charity such as CAFOD or Christian Aid. There is no requirement to do this however, and some may donate their money to non-Christian charities which help others.

For some Christians donating money can be hard, especially if they are poor themselves. They may still feel a duty to help others however. They could do this by donating their time or their expertise. They might for example volunteer in a charity shop or help at a homeless shelter. They could also help teach young previously homeless people how to cook, or provide knitted goods to help those in other countries.

The Salvation Army is a Christian denomination which places a great emphasis on helping those in need. They often raise money by playing in brass bands in town centres. This money is then used to provide homeless shelters, counselling for drug and alcohol abuse and basic equipment kits to help people who were homeless and are moving into rented accommodation.

Some Christians feel the need to be more involved in helping others. They might work for a charitable organisation full time. For some Christians their whole life becomes dedicated to helping those in need. Jackie Pullinger was a Christian who went to Hong Kong as a missionary. She was so distressed by the suffering of drug addicts there that she worked to set up homes where they could withdraw from the drugs and get help in readjusting to normal life. Some Christians get involved in political campaigns in order to try and bring about change which benefits those in need.

RESEARCH NOTE

Read the parable of The Sheep and the Goats in Matthew 25. What implications does this have for Christians about how they should behave?

FOR DEBATE

'When you mix politics and religion, you get politics.' Discuss this statement.

Should Christians get involved in political action, or should they leave politics to the politicians?

ACTIVITIES

Should the poor have to rely on charities to help them or should society be fairer to everyone in the first place?

Religion, poverty and wealth

The next two pages will help you to:

- explain why some ways of earning a living are not acceptable to Christians
- evaluate your own views about moral and immoral ways of earning a living.

AO1+AO2 *skills* **ACTIVITIES**

Make two lists: one showing jobs that you think are moral, the other showing those you think are immoral. Look at the lists again after reading these two pages. Do you think a Christian would agree with your lists? Make any additions or changes you think a Christian might make in a different coloured pen.

Many Christians do not approve of gambling.

Concept of moral and immoral

When people use the words **moral** and **immoral** they are usually talking about things which they consider to be good or bad, good or evil or right and wrong. These may be things which people just 'know' are right or wrong, or things which a religion says are right or wrong.

Moral and immoral occupations

Many people might have an instinctive idea of jobs which they would consider to be immoral because they hurt or exploit others. For Christians their concept of what jobs are immoral is also likely to be influenced by the Bible.

The Bible does not list moral and immoral occupations, but its teachings about how to treat others can be used to help determine whether a job would be immoral. One example is the teaching in the Bible against usury which might lead Christians to believe that working for a debt consolidation company (who charge higher than usual rates of interest to those whose loans have become unmanageable) would be immoral.

Some Christians use the second of the 'Two Great Commandments' in Mark as their guideline about whether an occupation is moral or immoral. This says people should love their neighbour as themselves. This might then imply that if an occupation could harm others then it would be immoral. This could be easily applied to occupations which directly cause harm to others, for example pornography, or gambling which causes most gamblers to lose money.

What is more difficult to assess is how far people should take this, for example should a Christian reject a job working for a fishing magazine because the same publisher also publishes pornography? Should they refuse to work for a major chocolate manufacturer because they buy cocoa beans in a way which exploits cocoa workers? Would working for a drug manufacturer which conducted human tests in LEDCs be acceptable? There are no straightforward answers to these questions, and individual Christians have to come to their own conclusions.

There are however occupations which clearly uphold the Great Commandments, and these might be deemed by Christians as moral. They are often jobs in the 'caring' professions, where the work carried out can be seen to have a direct impact on people's lives. They include teaching, medicine, social services and most **charity** work. Some other occupations might fall into this category as without them people's lives might be very difficult or dangerous. This might include refuse collectors, cleaners, and people working in the court systems, or the fire services.

Impacts of these teachings on believers

Although Christians will always try to live by the teachings of the Bible, there may be situations in which they find it very difficult to know what to do. The Bible might indicate that an occupation is immoral. This might be something which most people agree is immoral or it might be something rather different, like working with battery hens which the individual Christian might think was cruel. Sometimes people who have to earn a living and support their families may find that they have to compromise their beliefs in order to survive.

> **Mark 12:29–31**
>
> 'The most important one,' answered Jesus, 'is this: "Hear, O Israel, the Lord our God, the Lord is one. Love the Lord your God with all your heart and with all your soul and with all your mind and with all your strength." The second is this: "Love your neighbour as yourself." There is no commandment greater than these.'

AO2 skills ACTIVITIES

'Christians should be prepared to take any job rather than be unemployed.' Discuss this statement. You should include different, supported points of views and a personal viewpoint.

Remember and Reflect

The questions in this section are based on the work you have done throughout this Topic. Try to complete as many questions as you can.

The questions in set 1 are designed to test your factual recall and AO1 level skills (knowledge and understanding). The page numbers alongside the questions will help you to find information that might be useful for your answers. Use them to check against what you have written.

The questions in set 2 are more challenging, using AO2 level skills (use of evidence and reasoned argument to evaluate personal responses and differing viewpoints). Your answers many come from more than one part of the Topic.

AO1 Describe, explain and analyse, using knowledge and understanding

Find the answer on:

1 List three causes of poverty.	PAGE 126, 127
2 What is usury?	PAGE 127
3 Give two reasons why Christians might be unhappy with the poverty in LEDCs.	PAGE 126, 127
4 Explain why LEDCs are more likely to be harmed by natural disasters than MEDCs.	PAGE 127
5 Give one Biblical teaching about wealth and explain what it means.	PAGE 128
6 Why might Christians think being wealthy leads to temptation?	PAGE 128
7 Give one example of a Christian who has used their wealth to help others.	PAGE 129
8 Explain how the Christian Action on Poverty (CAP) practice of living on the minimum wage during Lent might help Christians develop empathy for the poor.	PAGE 129
9 Explain in 50 words what the Bible says about helping the poor.	PAGE 130, 131
10 Give the names of two Christian charities.	PAGE 130
11 What is a tithe?	PAGE 131
12 How might those with little money care for those in need?	PAGE 131
13 What does the Bible say about moral and immoral occupations?	PAGE 133
14 Construct a chart like the one below showing what Christians might consider moral and immoral occupations and why.	PAGE 133

Moral occupations	Why?	Immoral occupations	Why?

AO2 Use evidence and reasoned argument to express and evaluate personal responses, informed insights, and differing viewpoints

1 'It is the responsibility of LEDCs to sort out their own problems.' Discuss this statement. You should include different, supported points of view and a personal viewpoint. You must refer to Christianity in your answer.

2 Construct an argument showing the benefits of accumulating wealth so one can then help other people.

3 'People who gather great riches are selfish.' Discuss this statement. You should include different, supported points of view and a personal viewpoint. You must refer to Christianity in your answer.

4 Create a chart like the one below showing the advantages and disadvantages of charities helping people in need.

Advantages	Disadvantages

Now explain whether you think charities should help those in need or not.

5 'Giving money to charity is not doing enough to help those in need.' Discuss this statement. You should include different, supported points of view and a personal viewpoint. You must refer to Christianity in your answer.

6 Copy and complete the chart below to help you give supported evidence for or against the statements in the chart.

	How a Christian might respond	Evidence to support their views
'Any job is better than none.'		
'No Christian should ever work for a gambling organisation.'		
'I can't work in my local newsagent – it sells pornography.'		

Welcome to the Grade Studio

Grade Studio is here to help you improve your answers by working through typical questions you might find on an examination paper. For a full explanation of how this feature works and how exam questions are structured, see page 14. For a full explanation of Assessment Objectives and Levels of Response, see pages x–xi in the Introduction.

AO1 Question

Why might Christians give money to charity?

[6 marks]

Student's answer

Christians are nice people who want others to like them, so they will always give money to charity. Christians also believe that the Bible says they must give to charity.

Some Christians give money in church every Sunday when there is a collection so that the church can work to help others. They do this because Jesus praised people who helped others.

Comments

The candidate has given a satisfactory answer to the question. The opening sentence is very weak. There are two relevant points but neither is explained in any detail. In order to reach Level 3 the candidate needs to give more information and examples. The candidate could also use more technical terms from the specification to show the breadth of their knowledge and understanding.

Student's improved answer

Christians are nice people who want others to like them, so they will always give money to charity. Christians also believe that the Bible says they must give to charity.

Some Christians give money in church every Sunday when there is a collection so that the church can work to help others. They do this because Jesus praised people who helped others.

Some people, as well as giving to a weekly collection, may also give a tenth of their income to the church to help the less fortunate – this is called tithing. Charity has always been part of Christian life and teaching since the time of the deacons in Jerusalem who looked after the widows. Also, Jesus told the Parable of the Widow's Mite where a widow gave a tiny amount, but it was really all she had, as an example of how and why people should give to charity. He also told the rich young ruler to sell all his possessions and give the money to the poor. By giving money to charity, Christians are following Jesus' teaching and example.

Comments

This is now a good answer to the question. The candidate has shown a clear understanding of the question. There is good description and explanation of a variety of different reasons why Christians might give to charity. The candidate has shown some analysis. The information is presented clearly and there is good use of technical terms.

AO2 Question

'People must look after their family before they worry about the poor.' *Discuss this statement. You should include different, supported points of view and a personal viewpoint. You must refer to Christianity in your answer.* **[12 marks]**

Student's answer

The proverb says 'charity begins at home', so of course people should look after their own family first.

Some Christians might also say that their family is their first responsibility and so they must look after the needs of their family before they can worry about people outside of it. The Bible is clear about the responsibilty of parents towards their children, so the family must come first.

Comments

The candidate has given a limited answer to the question. There are two points but they both address the same point of view and neither is expanded. In order to reach Level 4 the candidate needs to give alternative viewpoints and also include a personal response.

Student's improved answer

The proverb says 'charity begins at home', so of course people should look after their own family first. Some Christians might also say that their family is their first responsibility and so they must look after the needs of their family before they can worry about people outside of it. The Bible is clear about the responsibilty of parents towards their children, so the family must come first.

Some people, on the other hand, might think that because of the amount of suffering, disease and poverty in the world, as Christians they have an obligation to look after the poor. Jesus told his followers to look after the poor and not to concern themselves with their own wellbeing. He asked his Disciples to leave their family and follow him and put others before their family. The parable of The Sheep and the Goats makes it clear that God will judge people by how they helped others who are in need. I think the statement is correct.

My personal opinion is that Christians have to strike a balance between the two positions. Of course, they have to look after their family but, if they are thinking of spending money on things that are simply luxuries, they need to be concerned about doing something for the poor first.

Comments

This is now a good answer to the question. The candidate has shown a clear understanding of the question and has presented a range of views supported by evidence and argument. The answer explains Christian views, amongst others, and includes a personal viewpoint, which is also supported.

These specimen answers provide an outline of how you could construct your response. Space does not allow us to give a full response. You will need to provide more detail in your actual exam responses.

Topic 10: Religion, peace and justice

The Big Picture

In this Topic, you will be addressing Christian beliefs and teachings about:

- the attitudes people have to war
- violence and pacifism
- crime and punishment
- how ideas about social justice are shaped by belief and the consequences they have for behaviour.

You will also think about your own feelings and responses to these questions and issues.

DID YOU KNOW?

- Over 80,000 people are in jail in the UK.
- Most crimes reported to the police do not end with a prosecution.
- Millions of pounds are spent on weapons every second.
- Christians differ greatly in their views on war and peace.

KEY WORDS

capital punishment Executing a criminal convicted of murder and other crimes.

conscientious objector Someone who refuses to fight in a war on the basis of their conscience.

judge The Christian idea of God acting as a judge to determine whether a person goes to Heaven or Hell after death.

Just War theory The belief that wars can be morally justified if they follow certain criteria.

justice Fairness in society and the world.

nuclear pacifism Belief that the use of nuclear weapons can never be justified.

pacifism The belief that peace should be the central value that people pursue.

proportionality The belief that force can only be met with equal force.

Quaker A member of the Christian denomination also known as the Religious Society of Friends.

revenge Seeking to repay a wrong by getting recompense.

sin An act which goes against God's will.

social justice The belief that people should be treated fairly and with respect in a society.

social injustice Where people may be denied rights as a consequence of poverty or discrimination.

violence The use of physical force, with the intention to harm.

HERE RESTS IN HONORED GLORY
A COMRADE IN ARMS
KNOWN BUT TO GOD

The gravestone of an unknown soldier.

 **GET STARTED**

'Christian ideas about peace are irrelevant to today's world as they owe their origins to the Bible.' Do you agree or disagree with this statement? Give reasons. Do a survey to find out what people think about this question and why.

What attitudes are there to war?

The next two pages will help you to:

- examine the attitudes people have to war
- examine how ideas such as the Just War influence people's attitudes to war.

AO1 skills **ACTIVITIES**

Write a list of films about, or containing war, or fighting in them. Why have you chosen the stories you have? Do they show war as having a point or being always wrong? Share your ideas with another couple and then present your ideas to the class so that they can then form the basis of a mind map to be put into your notes.

Soldiers patrolling in Iraq.

What is the point of war?

What is the point of war? One famous song of the 1970s called *War*, sung by Edwin Starr, asked the question what war was good for and came to the conclusion the answer was 'absolutely nothing'. When you think of the consequences that war can have on the people involved in it, it is easy to see why a person might think it can never bring any good. These include:

- **Death:** millions were killed in wars in the last century.

- **Destruction of property and land:** this makes it difficult to re-start the economy of the nation after fighting.

- **Disease:** this often follows due to damage to food, water and medical supplies, which allows diseases like cholera to spread.

- **Mental illness:** for both the participants in the fighting and those exposed to attack, mental health issues might follow. Some soldiers might suffer from what is called post-traumatic stress disorder, where even years later, they may have flashbacks about incidents that occurred when they were fighting.

What are the attitudes of Christians to war?

Some Christians believe that war is often the result of the sin, the evil choices of people made in direct contradiction to the will of God. However, some think that on occasion, it may still be necessary to fight in order to deal with a greater evil rather than not. Many Christians believe that war can only be fought if certain moral principles are followed.

Many Christians believe that the rejection of war and **violence** is what Jesus stressed in the gospels. They believe in **pacifism** – the belief that peace should be the central value people pursue; this normally means that war and violence are seen as unacceptable. They quote such sayings of Jesus as 'for all who draw the sword will die by the sword' (Matthew 26:52b).

They may say that no Christian believed in fighting for the government or in war until the Romans officially adopted Christianity and it became the religion of the Empire.

What is meant by the Just War theory?

Some people feel that the only justification for war would be if they were defending, either their own country or another country. Britain went to war against Germany in 1939 as they were seeking to defend Poland against being invaded.

Some wars might need to be fought, so how could they be seen as morally necessary? In a book called the *Summa Theologiae*, the Christian thinker St Thomas Aquinas (1225–74), wrote about a theory of **Just War**, a war that it is better to fight than not. Some of these principles preceded Aquinas and others were developed later. To be a Just War, the war must follow certain criteria. Here are six that are very important:

1   The war must be fought for a just cause. There must be a just or moral reason, such as defending a nation under attack or trying to stop a tyranny.

2   There must be controlled violence. Every effort must be made to make sure that as little violence is used as possible. Any use of force that is more than the enemy can or has used is seen as immoral.

3   A war can be fought if it is believed that a greater evil would exist if the war were not fought. People argue that if Britain and her allies had not taken on the Nazi regime of Adolf Hitler, then far greater evil would have happened.

4   In order for a war to be just, it must be in the control of the politicians and not just dominated by the military in the war zone. They can take only minor decisions, the politicians should be able to take the most important.

5   The force used in the war should be proportional. By **proportionality**, it means that the amount of force should not be excessive. The military should also try to avoid injuring innocent civilians.

6   Only the military should be involved in the fighting of the war and they should seek to avoid the damage of property and others.

AO2 skills **ACTIVITIES**

'The consequences of war are always so negative that there can be no good reasons for going to war.' What do you think? What might a Christian say? Give reasons for your answers, showing that you have thought about it from more than one point of view.

What do Christians believe about violence and pacifism?

The next two pages will help you to:

- explain attitudes to violence and pacifism
- examine how these ideas influence Christian behaviour.

Attitudes to violence

In the earliest parts of the Bible, the attitudes to **violence** are quite stark. In the book of Exodus 15:3, there is a psalm that celebrates the defeat of the Egyptians. Look at the ideas it contains 'The Lord is a warrior; the Lord his name.' For many people, the idea of God as a warrior is problematic. How could he fight on one side or the other?

There are many different attitudes to violence amongst Christians. Whilst some believe that violence can be justified at the national level by fighting in a war that they believe is just, they may be less willing to endorse violence in other contexts. They might make a distinction between violence and force. Violence is destructive whereas force might be about trying to restrict a person from behaving violently, such as when a police officer might use force to stop a person from using violence.

Some Christians believe that Jesus' teaching in the Sermon on the Mount tells them that they should avoid personally seeking **revenge**, such as when Jesus tells his followers to offer the other cheek if they are struck (Matthew 5:39). However, they might well say that these ideas only apply to individual Christians and not to entire countries.

Many Christians emphasise the importance of order in a society being the will of God and that as a consequence, Christians should try to support the governments of the world trying to take order. Many also say that where governments use violence in such practices as torture, this should be addressed, as that abuse of another human being clearly contradicts the idea that all people are made in the image of God.

AO1 skills ACTIVITIES

What do you think are good reasons for war? Try to list as many of these as you can and then share your lists with a partner and then as a class.

The death of the Egyptians in the Red Sea from a 10th-century Bible.

Attitudes to pacifism

Pacifism is the belief that peace should be the central value that people pursue, this usually involves the belief that the use of violence to fight in a war or to defend yourself is not right. However, when the Emperor Constantine accepted Christianity, the Roman Empire began to convince Christians that they had to fight in order to protect their faith. For example, he and subsequent leaders of Christian countries have put the Cross on their shields or have seen that there is a spiritual dimension to fighting by providing priests to support the troops. Down the centuries, the Christian church has often argued for a **Just War** theory, though there are many people to this day who campaign for non-violent resistance.

Some Christians have made a distinction between pacifism and what they call **nuclear pacifism**. A nuclear pacifist believes that the use of an atomic weapon can never be justified as the consequences of the use of such a weapon would never be equal to the evil that needed to be defeated. They do not necessarily rule out use of force in other ways.

What is a Quaker approach to war?

The Religious Society of Friends, or **Quakers** as they are also known, have been committed to pacifism from their origins. They believe that this is what Jesus required. One of the famous statements of their principles is called the Quaker Peace Testimony. It was written at a time when the king, Charles II, accused them of being involved in plots against his reign:

66 *We utterly deny all outward wars and strife and fighting with outward weapons for any end or under any pretense whatsoever; this is our testimony to the whole world... The Spirit of Christ by which we are guided is not changeable, so as once to command us from a thing of evil and again to move us into it; and we certainly know and testify to the world that the Spirit of Christ which leads us into all truth will never move us to fight and war against any man with outward weapons, neither for the Kingdom of Christ nor for the kingdoms of this world... therefore we cannot learn war anymore.* 99

To this day, Quakers are conscientious objectors, that is they refuse to fight in wars. However, they may be willing to be involved in the medical care needed for those caught up in conflict.

Some Christians believe that pacifism is naïve in that it seems to assume that human beings can act in a selfless way. They believe that Christian pacifism does not think about the sin that pervades all human beings and their politics. Other Christians believe that pacifist movements like the Christian Campaign for Nuclear Disarmament are too linked to party politics which they feel is not appropriate for Christians.

Many Christians extend these beliefs about pacifism to all aspects of their life. They do not believe that violence can ever be justified. However, others may say that when Jesus threw the money-lenders out of the Temple in Jerusalem (Matthew 21:10–17) he was acting in a violent manner and that sometimes violence may be justified.

AO2 skills ACTIVITIES

'The Just War is irrelevant to the 21st century.' What do you think? What might Christians say? Show that you have thought about it from several points of view.

Crime and punishment

A prisoner in his cell.

The concept of justice

Justice can be defined as 'just behaviour or treatment'. For Christians, the idea of justice comes from a belief that all people are created in the image of God and should therefore be treated with dignity and respect. Some Christians relate the idea of justice to the idea of love in action, making sure that all are cared for and protected.

Christians believe that justice is an important quality in a society. The prophet Isaiah, for example, condemns the false justice and lack of care in Israel. Jesus' emphasis on not personally seeking **revenge** is seen by some Christians as a command to individuals and not to whole societies. Paul in Romans 13:1–6 talks about the important role of government upholding the rule of law, which Christians should support. Ultimately Christians believe that however good human justice is, it will not be of the same quality as that which God will demonstrate at the final judgement, when all people will be judged.

What are the aims of punishment?

There are many different reasons why criminals are punished. Here are some which are used to justify the idea of why it is just to seek punishment: revenge, vindication (punishing to uphold the idea of law), and reformation (using it as a way to improve someone) protection and deterrence.

Beliefs and responses to the treatment of criminals

Christians believe that criminals should be punished for their crimes, but it is also important that they are treated appropriately and fairly. Some Christians, such as the 18th-century **Quaker**, Elizabeth Fry, were actively involved in improving prisons so that prisoners had access to good food, education and were being treated well.

Some Christians have been involved in prison visiting and helping to run religious services in jails as they feel that Jesus' parable of The Sheep and the Goats in Matthew 25 explicitly mentions prisoners as one group that the followers of Jesus should be concerned about. Other Christians are concerned that the rights of the victims of crime and their needs are not always met.

Attitudes towards capital punishment

For some people, murder is a crime that should not be punished by a prison sentence but by execution. This is known as **capital punishment**. Although banned in the European Union, it is still practised in many countries such as in some states of the USA, where Christians are divided over whether it should be used. Some people believe that the crime of murder, or taking away life, is a violation of the will of God, who alone should take life. Therefore they believe that it needs this ultimate punishment.

Other Christians say that it is impossible to have a completely foolproof conviction and that to execute someone is unfair as it cannot be guaranteed that justice is being done. They refer to the principles of loving your neighbour and your enemy which Jesus taught, which they believe are not possible to reconcile with execution.

Some Christians have been actively involved in the campaign to stop capital punishment. One of the most well known is Sister Helen Prejean, an American nun who has dedicated her life to caring for people awaiting execution on Death Row. Her life was dramatised in the film, *Dead Man Walking* (1995), which showed some of the dilemmas she faced while standing up for the rights and dignity of those about to be executed.

The use of capital punishment also means that the society has to employ someone as an executioner and for many Christians that would be an unacceptable job as it would inevitably involve the taking of life. They say that God alone should be the **judge** and that for a human to have the power to take life is a violation of the created order.

AO2 skills **ACTIVITIES**

'A just world is impossible and therefore we should not even attempt to try to get one.' What do you think of this statement? What might Christians say? Refer in detail to Christian teachings to make your case.

What do Christians think about social injustice?

What are social justice and injustice?

Social justice is the belief that people should be treated fairly and with respect in a society, that they all should have equal access to housing, education and have the same human rights. **Social injustice** is where they may be denied those rights as a consequence of poverty or discrimination.

Christian beliefs about justice in the world

The world we live in often lacks justice and many people are not treated fairly. There are many ways in which humans can discriminate and use this as a reason to be unfair, such as reasons of race, religion, sex, sexuality, wealth or class for example.

Christians believe that God created all people.

 **ACTIVITIES**

'The world is never fair and never will be. We can do nothing about this.' What do you think about this statement? Give reasons for your answers.

> **Genesis 1:27**
> *So God created man in his own image, in the image of God he created him; male and female he created them.*

> **Galatians 3:28**
> *There is neither Jew nor Greek, slave nor free, male nor female, for you are all one in Christ Jesus.*

Christians point to sin as the reason why there are so many examples of a lack of social justice. Sin is rebellion against God, the deliberate choosing of ways of behaviour that are selfish and liable to hurt the person doing them and the people around them. Christ's crucifixion is for Christians a reminder of the consequence of sin – many believe that Christ's death paid the price of sin, which had cut off human beings from God and each other.

Jesus' parables stressed the idea of fairness and his personal treatment of women as well as members of other races should be an example of how to show love to different types of people. The Old Testament is full of the works of prophets calling for justice such as Isaiah in this passage:

> **Isaiah 58:10**
>
> *...if you spend yourselves in behalf of the hungry*
> *and satisfy the needs of the oppressed,*
> *then your light will rise in the darkness,*
> *and your night will become like the noonday.*

Great reforms in the UK such as the abolition of slavery, the introduction of free education and the development of the National Health Service can all be traced back to the involvement of Christians seeking a better world due to their beliefs.

The prophet Micah had a vision of a peaceful world beyond warfare and conflict:

> **Micah 4:3**
>
> *He will judge between many peoples*
> *and will settle disputes for strong nations far and wide.*
> *They will beat their swords into ploughshares*
> *and their spears into pruning hooks.*
> *Nation will not take up sword against nation,*
> *nor will they train for war anymore.*

What does the New Testament teach about justice?

Justice is one of the most important aspects of Jesus' teaching and there are examples of this through the gospels:

> **Matthew 5:9**
>
> *Blessed are the peacemakers, for they will be called sons of God.*

> **Matthew 25:43–44**
>
> *You have heard that it was said, 'Love your neighbour and hate your enemy.'*
> *But I tell you: Love your enemies and pray for those who persecute you.*

How do you respond to these sayings of Jesus? Some Christians believe there will only be a just society if people try to live by this code of love and forgiveness. The early Christian leader Paul wrote 'If your enemy is hungry, feed him; if he is thirsty, give him something to drink. In doing this, you will heap burning coals on his head. Do not be overcome by evil, but overcome evil with good' (Romans 8:20b–21). From these teachings Christians have developed many principles which have changed the world in which we all live.

It is the influence of such teachings as these which led Christians such as William Wilberforce (1759–1833), a British politician, who successfully opposed slavery and Martin Luther King Jr (1929–68), a Baptist minister who lead a campaign of non-violent protest against racism in the USA.

AO2 skills ACTIVITIES

'Christian teachings show that a perfect world is not possible and therefore Christians should spend their time preparing for heaven, not worrying about life on this planet.' What do you think? What might Christians believe? Try to include a diversity of opinions in your answers.

Remember and Reflect

The questions in this section are based on the work you have done throughout this Topic. Try to complete as many questions as you can.

The questions in set 1 are designed to test your factual recall and AO1 level skills (knowledge and understanding). The page numbers alongside the questions will help you to find information that might be useful for your answers. Use them to check against what you have written.

The questions in set 2 are more challenging, using AO2 level skills (use of evidence and reasoned argument to evaluate personal responses and differing viewpoints). Your answers many come from more than one part of the Topic.

AO1 Describe, explain and analyse, using knowledge and understanding

Find the answer on:

#	Question	Find the answer on:
1	Explain what Just War and proportionality means.	PAGE 141
2	Explain some of the consequences of war.	PAGE 140, 141
3	Why do Christians believe the Old Testament is important in helping them develop their views about justice?	PAGE 142, 144
4	Explain, giving examples, some of the teachings about war in the Old Testament.	PAGE 142, 144
5	Explain, giving examples, the teaching you will find in the New Testament about justice.	PAGE 141–144
6	Explain what pacifism and nuclear pacifism means.	PAGE 143
7	Explain what Christians mean by 'being made in the image of God'.	PAGE 142
8	Give three reasons why a Christian might be a pacifist.	PAGE 142, 143
9	Write a sentence to explain justice.	PAGE 144
10	Give three examples of why punishment is seen as important.	PAGE 145
11	Write down one argument for and one against capital punishment that Christians might use.	PAGE 145
12	Outline three reasons for a war to be declared just.	PAGE 141
13	What is meant by social justice and social injustice?	PAGE 146
14	Give examples of ways in which Christians have tried to reduce social injustice.	PAGE 146, 147
15	Give examples of the Christian teachings that have inspired Christians to work for social justice.	PAGE 146, 147

AO2 Use evidence and reasoned argument to express and evaluate personal responses, informed insights, and differing viewpoints

1 Answer the following, giving as much detail as possible. You should give at least three reasons to support your response and also show that you have taken into account opposite opinions.
   a *Christians should not support the idea of a Just War, considering the teaching of the New Testament.*
   b *Do you think Christian teaching contained in the Bible is relevant to the wars of today's world?*
   c *Do you feel that pacifism is unrealistic, considering the sin in people's lives?*
   d *What would you say are the essential things a Christian has to believe about war?*

2 'There can never be agreement between Christians about war.' Do you agree? What might Christians think? Show that you have thought about several points of view in your answer.

3 'Nuclear pacifism is not workable.' Do you agree with this statement? What might Christians think? Show that you have thought about several points of view in your answer.

4 'Capital punishment is totally against the teaching of Jesus.' Do you agree? What might Christians think? Show that you have thought about several points of view in your answer.

5 'Punishment should fit the crime.' How might this work? Would it be fair to do so? What might a Christian think about this?

Welcome to the Grade Studio

Grade Studio is here to help you improve your answers by working through typical questions you might find on an examination paper. For a full explanation of how this feature works and how exam questions are structured, see page 14. For a full explanation of Assessment Objectives and Levels of Response, see pages x–xi in the Introduction.

AO1 Question

What are Christian attitudes towards war?   [6 marks]

Student's answer

Student's answer	Comments
Christians are pacifists and believe that all war is wrong because Jesus was a pacifist. Some Christians believe that there are occasions such as a Just War which meet certain conditions and when it is right to fight in order to protect people. An example could be self defence.	The candidate has given a satisfactory answer to the question. There are two main points but only one of them, about Just War, has any valid explanation, but that is brief and does not add much to the answer. In order to reach Level 3 the candidate needs to give more information and examples. The candidate could also use more technical terms from the specification to show the breadth of their knowledge and understanding.

Student's improved answer

Student's improved answer	Comments
Christians are pacifists and believe that all war is wrong because Jesus was a pacifist. Some Christians believe that there are occasions such as a Just War which meet certain conditions and when it is right to fight in order to protect people or in self defence. Another could be that it is right to fight as long as civilians are not harmed. Some Christians say that there are examples in the Bible of wars that were fought with God's approval and help. Some Christians have believed it is right to fight in a Holy War, which is fought to protect the Christian religion. However there are some Christians such as Quakers (The Religious Society of Friends) who are total pacifists and will not fight under any circumstances. They follow Jesus' teaching of turning the other cheek rather then fighting back.	This is now a good answer to the question. The candidate has shown a clear understanding of the question. There is good description and explanation of a variety of different attitudes towards war. The candidate has shown some analysis in dealing with the Quakers. The information is presented clearly and there is good use of technical terms.

AO2 Question

'All people must be pacifists.' Discuss this statement. You should include different, supported points of view and a personal viewpoint. You must refer to Christianity in your answer. **[12 marks]**

Student's answer

Some Christians say that all people must be pacifists because they believe that Jesus was a pacifist and never hurt anybody.

Other Christians believe that the commandment says 'do not kill' and that therefore any fighting must be wrong because people risk being killed. Jesus told people to turn the other cheek when they were hit and not to seek revenge, so even fighting in self defence is wrong. Two wrongs don't make a right.

Comments

The candidate has given a limited answer to the question. There are two relevant points but one is a matter of opinion and the other is a common misinterpretation resulting in a misunderstanding. In order to reach Level 4 the candidate needs to give alternative viewpoints and also include a personal response.

Student's improved answer

Some Christians say that all people must be pacifists because they believe that Jesus was a pacifist and never hurt anybody. Other Christians believe that the commandment says 'do not kill' and that therefore any fighting must be wrong because people risk being killed. Jesus told people to turn the other cheek when they were hit and not to seek revenge, so even fighting in self defence is wrong. Two wrongs don't make a right.

Comments

This is now a good answer to the question. The candidate has shown a clear understanding of the question and has presented a range of views supported by evidence and argument. The answer explains Christian views, amongst others, and includes a personal viewpoint, which is also supported.

Some people, on the other hand, might think that there are circumstances, such as during a Just War, when it is necessary for Christians and others to fight. To do nothing would be wrong and would let evil win. Christian thinkers have devised some rules for a war which is just or right such as self defence, ensuring civilians are not hurt, only using a reasonable amount of force and making sure the war will produce a better situation than existed before the conflict. My personal opinion is that it is not easy to decide whether to be a total pacifist or not.

There may be circumstances, such as during the Second World War, where people have a duty to fight in order to protect their country from being overrun by evil. I could not stand by and let my family be killed I would have to do something to stop it which would mean I had to fight. So I think it would be great if all people were pacifists because there would be peace everywhere, but as they are not, it will sometimes be necessary to fight which is the less evil thing to do than allow evil to win.

These specimen answers provide an outline of how you could construct your response. Space does not allow us to give a full response. You will need to provide more detail in your actual exam responses.

Topic 11: Religion and equality

The Big Picture

In this Topic, you will be addressing Christian beliefs and teachings about:

- the principle of equality
- attitudes towards racism
- attitudes towards gender
- attitudes towards other religions
- forgiveness and reconciliation.

You will also think about your own feelings and responses to these questions and issues.

DID YOU KNOW?

- Some Christians say that the Bible teaches that everyone is equal in the sight of God.

- Christians believe that racial discrimination is always wrong. Many Christians devote their lives to fighting racism and other discrimination.

- Some Christians believe that God created men and women to have different roles; others think that they should have the right to choose. Some believe that only men should become priests, but there are now many women priests and ministers. Members of the Church of England disagree about whether women should be allowed to become bishops.

- Some Christians think Christianity is the only true religion and that all other religions are false. Many Christians are committed to evangelism, while others work to develop interfaith understanding. Some Christians support the ecumenical movement, helping Christians of different denominations to understand each other better.

GET STARTED

'Women still not paid as much as men!' Are you surprised that this is still the case in modern society? What do you think are the reasons for this? Is this unfair?

There is now far greater equality between men and women in work.

KEY WORDS

discrimination Unjust or prejudicial treatment because of race, age, gender or disability.

ecumenical Different Christian denominations working together.

equality Treating people as equals regardless of gender, race or religious beliefs.

Eucharist The Christian ceremony commemorating the Last Supper, in which bread and wine are consecrated and consumed.

evangelism Persuading others to share your faith.

forgiveness Forgiving someone for something they have done wrong.

prejudice Making judgements not based on reason or actual experience.

proselytising Trying to convert people from their religion to yours.

racism Prejudice, discrimination or ill treatment against someone because of their race.

reconciliation Restoring friendly relations.

repentance Sincere regret or remorse from one's actions.

sexism Prejudice, stereotyping or discrimination, typically against women, on the basis of sex.

What is equality?

Equality

The two words which are frequently used when talking about **equality** are **prejudice** and **discrimination**.

- **prejudice:** an idea or feeling which one person holds and which affects another person.
- **discrimination:** action based on prejudice.

On 10 December 1948 the General Assembly of the United Nations formally adopted the United Nations Declaration of Human Rights. The first two articles state that everyone in the world should have exactly the same rights and freedoms:

- **Article 1:** All human beings are born free and equal in dignity and rights. They are endowed with reason and conscience and should act towards one another in a spirit of brotherhood.
- **Article 2:** Everyone is entitled to all the rights and freedoms set forth in this Declaration, without distinction of any kind, such as race, colour, sex, language, religion, political or other opinion, national or social origin, property, birth or other status.

Despite the Declaration the media shows every day that thousands of people suffer from inequality and discrimination.

What does the Bible teach about equality?

Christians are told that all humans are made 'in the image of God' (Genesis 1:27). They believe that all humans matter to God, regardless of race, gender, ability, wealth or skills, and that all who pray to God will be listened to and treated without favouritism. As a result of God's attitude to humans, they should treat others with the same respect.

Christians also believe that they should treat others in the way they would wish to be treated: 'Love your neighbour as yourself' (Luke 10:27b).

The next two pages will help you to:

- examine the principle of equality
- examine Biblical teachings about equality
- evaluate Christian attitudes towards equality.

Eleanor Roosevelt (1884–1962) was the first chairperson of the UN Human Rights commission which produced the Declaration of Human Rights.

 **ACTIVITIES**

Keep a list for a day. On your list make two columns, one of things which happen that you think are fair and one of things which you think are unfair. Compare your list with a partner. Which events do you disagree on?

MUST THINK ABOUT!

Some people say that discrimination = prejudice + power.

Christian attitudes towards equality

When it comes to specific teaching on equality there are passages in both the Old and New Testaments of the Bible:

> **Leviticus 19:33–34**
>
> *When an alien lives with you in your land, do not ill-treat him. The alien living with you must be treated as one of your native-born. Love him as yourself, for you were aliens in Egypt. I am the Lord your God.*

> **Galatians 3:28**
>
> *There is neither Jew nor Greek, slave nor free, male nor female, for you are all one in Christ Jesus.*

The first passage refers to the time that the Israelites were slaves in Egypt. However, although the second passage is often taken to mean that, according to Christianity, everyone is equal; some scholars believe that it simply says that all Christians are equal.

There are also teachings about not showing favouritism to particular people.

> **James 2:1**
>
> *My brothers, as believers in our glorious Lord Jesus Christ, don't show favouritism.*

> **Acts 10:34–35**
>
> *Then Peter began to speak: 'I now realise how true it is that God does not show favouritism but accepts men from every nation who fear him and do what is right.'*

Christian views on prejudice and discrimination

Christians believe that they should follow the example of Jesus, therefore all people should be treated in the same way. Jesus healed the son of a Roman centurion, even though the Romans were hated; he showed respect for women, who were generally seen as less important than men; and he made a Samaritan the hero of one of his most famous parables, even though the people of Samaria were not respected by the Jews.

The parable of The Good Samaritan:

> **Luke 10:30–35a**
>
> *Jesus said: 'A man was going down from Jerusalem to Jericho, when he fell into the hands of robbers. They stripped him of his clothes, beat him and went away, leaving him half dead. A priest happened to be going down the same road, and when he saw the man, he passed by on the other side. So too, a Levite, when he came to the place and saw him, passed by on the other side. But a Samaritan, as he travelled, came where the man was; and when he saw him, he took pity on him. He went to him and bandaged his wounds, pouring on oil and wine. Then he put the man on his own donkey, took him to an inn and took care of him. The next day he took out two silver coins and gave them to the innkeeper. "Look after him," he said.'*

RESEARCH NOTE

Find a copy of the United Nations Declaration of Human Rights on the Internet. Read the preamble and then explain, in your own words, why the Declaration was written.

FOR DEBATE

'All animals are born equal, but some are more equal than others.' Discuss what this quotation from George Orwell's book *Animal Farm* means. Decide whether you agree with it and explain your opinions.

ACTIVITIES

'Not everyone is equal.' Do you agree? How might a Christian respond to this statement?

Christian attitudes towards racism and gender

The next two pages will help you to:

- examine Christian views on racism and sexism
- evaluate different Christian responses to racism and sexism.

Christianity and racism

There have been many occasions in the history of Christianity when the behaviour of individuals or groups of Christians would be described as racist.

- During the Crusades thousands of people across Europe and the Middle East were killed in the name of Christianity.

- During their voyages of exploration in the 16th century, Spain invaded South America. Tens of thousands of the inhabitants were killed in attempts to force them to convert to Christianity. At the same time the Spanish navy took all their wealth.

- The slave plantations of the Caribbean and the American Deep South were mostly owned by Christians. Slavery was abolished in the United States of America at the end of the Civil War in 1865.

There are some passages in the New Testament which have been used to support slavery.

> **1 Corinthians 7:21–22**
> *Were you a slave when called? Do not be concerned about it. Even if you can gain your freedom, make use of your present condition now more than ever. For whoever was called in the Lord as a slave is a freed person belonging to the Lord, just as whoever was free when called is a slave of Christ.*

However, the Christian Church today condemns any form of slavery. In 1948, in South Africa, the Prime Minister, the Rev. Daniel François Malan, introduced the legislation known as apartheid. Under these laws people were separated by their skin colour: black, white or coloured. This was supported by the Dutch Reformed Church of which Malan was a minister.

It was not until 1994 that apartheid was finally abolished in South Africa.

This memorial in Soweto, South Africa, honours the memory of Hector Pieterson (1946–76) who was killed during student riots against the apartheid regime.

ACTIVITIES

In pairs, write down as many different types of discrimination as you can think of. Remember, sometimes discrimination can be a good thing. Share your list with a group and then with the whole class. How many different types did you think of? How many of these types are positive?

RESEARCH NOTE

Research the first four Crusades and produce a PowerPoint presentation about them.

Christianity and sexism

Sexism is a form of **prejudice** based on gender, typically against women. In the past, many people felt that men and women possessed different skills, and this has resulted in their being treated differently. The Church has often been accused of being sexist. The language used in the Church seems to be in favour of men and God and is almost always referred to as being male.

There are several passages in the New Testament where St Paul appears to be saying that women are inferior to men.

> **1 Corinthians 14:34–35**
>
> *Women should remain silent in the churches. They are not allowed to speak, but must be in submission, as the Law says. If they want to enquire about something, they should ask their own husbands at home; for it is disgraceful for a woman to speak in the church.*

> **1 Corinthians 11:3**
>
> *Now I want you to realise that the head of every man is Christ, and the head of the woman is man, and the head of Christ is God.*

This has led to a traditional view that men should go out to work to provide for the family while women bring up children and run the home. However, many Christians now feel that men and women should be given equal opportunities and responsibilities in the workplace and at home.

The role of women in the Church

The Christian Church has been very slow in changing its position in relation to women. In the Roman Catholic Church, women are not accepted as priests as it is felt that only men should say the words spoken by Jesus that are repeated during the Mass. It is also thought that because God came to earth in the form of a man – Jesus – his representatives on earth should only be men and the 12 apostles chosen by Jesus were all men. St Paul also taught that women 'should be silent'.

However, many other denominations have long accepted women in their ministry. Methodists, Baptists and others allow both men and women to be ministers, to preach and to have equal responsibility. The Church of England accepted women as vicars in 1994. Some Anglicans disagree with this and have not been comfortable with women taking over their parish (church area).

In recent years many Christians have argued that women should have an equal role in worship and the priesthood not just on grounds of **equality** but because of what happened in the early Church.

> **Romans 16:3–4**
>
> *Greet Priscilla and Aquila, my fellow workers in Christ Jesus. They risked their lives for me. Not only I but all the churches of the Gentiles are grateful to them. Greet also the church that meets at their house.*

RESEARCH NOTE

Perhaps the most famous Christian campaigner against racism is Martin Luther King Jr. Find out about his life and work.

A female priest.

MUST THINK ABOUT!

There are female Anglican vicars, but no female Anglican bishops as yet.

AO2 skills ACTIVITIES

'If men and women are equal then women can become priests.' Do you agree? How might a Christian respond to this statement?

Attitudes towards other religions

The next two pages will help you to:

- examine Christian views about other religions
- understand what is meant by missionary work, evangelism and ecumenism.

Christianity and other religions

Christianity is a religion that believes in evangelism. This means that Christians believe that they should try to encourage everyone to become members of their faith. This is because of the commission Jesus gave to the disciples:

> **Matthew 28:16–20a**
>
> *Then the eleven disciples went to Galilee, to the mountain where Jesus had told them to go. When they saw him, they worshipped him; but some doubted. Then Jesus came to them and said, 'All authority in heaven and on earth has been given to me. Therefore go and make disciples of all nations, baptising them in the name of the Father and of the Son and of the Holy Spirit, and teaching them to obey everything I have commanded you.'*

ACTIVITIES

Write down three things you believe to be true. Explain to a partner how you came to believe the statements were true and what 'true' means in each case.

So although Christians believe that everyone should have the right to practise their own religion many also believe that only Christianity has the complete truth about God: 'the Church still has the obligation and also the sacred right to evangelise all men' (Catechism of the Roman Catholic Church). There are other Christians who believe that if people are following their own religion then they are also worshipping God.

Missionary work

The commission to spread the gospel, or evangelise, is taken seriously by many Christians, who feel that they should become involved in missionary work – bringing the Christian message to people in their own country and all over the world. For hundreds of years Christians travelled around the world as missionaries. These people felt that, as Christians, it was their duty to convert as many people as possible. They believed that it was only by becoming Christians that people had a chance of reaching heaven when they died.

Christians involved in missionary work feel that it is essential to give everyone the opportunity to follow the Christian faith in order to know God.

MUST THINK ABOUT!

Islam and Christianity are proselytising religions. However, some other religions such as Hinduism and Judaism do not generally encourage converts because they believe that people can serve God through a different religion.

> **John 14:6**
>
> *Jesus answered: 'I am the way and the truth and the life. No one comes to the Father except by me.'*

There are still missionary societies today. However, while they are still concerned with spreading the Christian message, their main purpose is to help people in developing countries by following the example of Jesus.

Ecumenism

This is the name given to the movement that tries to unite different Christians. There are hundreds of different Christian groups and often they have different ways of practising their faith. Many denominations – mostly Protestant and Orthodox – meet as members of the World Council of Churches in order to celebrate the fact that all confess the Lord Jesus Christ, according to the Holy Scriptures, as God and Saviour. The spirit of ecumenism has been encouraged by many of the Asian and African Churches, which have demonstrated great courage in the face of persecution.

The motto of the Church Mission Society.

Several Christian communities have been established to help members of different denominations come together to worship.

Taizé

In 1940 Roger Schutz founded a religious community of monks at Taizé in France that sheltered Jewish refugees escaping Nazi Germany until 1942. When the Nazis occupied France, Roger had to leave but returned at the end of the war, initially caring for German prisoners of war, practising the Christian belief of forgiveness and **reconciliation**.

Taizé is a place of pilgrimage particularly for young people from all over the world and, as an **ecumenical** community, works to break down barriers between Christian denominations. The monks also are from different churches and different countries.

Young people camp in the fields, join in daily worship and help with practical work in the kitchens and on the farms. Worship includes simple songs in Latin, French, German and English. There is time for meditation and reflection allowing young people to develop self-awareness of what is in their heart and to listen to God. Times of group discussion encourage listening skills and a chance to discuss the challenges of being a young Christian. Living a simpler monastic life without television and luxuries helps people find a meaning to life and to decide what is really important.

AO2 skills **ACTIVITIES**

'All Christians should forget their differences and worship together.' Do you agree? How might a Christian respond to this statement?

Forgiveness and reconciliation

The next two pages will help you to:

- examine Christian beliefs about forgiveness and reconciliation
- understand how these beliefs affect Christians
- evaluate the importance of these beliefs for Christians.

Coventry Cathedral was rebuilt after being bombed during the Second World War (1939–45). It is often thought of as being a place of reconciliation.

Christian beliefs about forgiveness and reconciliation

Forgiveness

Forgiveness is when we forgive people for something which they have done wrong. **Reconciliation** is the ending of a dispute or the restoring of a good relationship between people who have been in dispute.

It can be hard to forgive someone, but Christians are encouraged to do so. Jesus said many things about forgiveness (see Matthew 5:43–45).

Jesus demonstrated this teaching about forgiveness in the Parable of the Woman Taken in Adultery:

Matthew 5:43–45

You have heard that it was said, 'Love your neighbour and hate your enemy.' But I tell you: Love your enemies and pray for those who persecute you, that you may be sons of your Father in heaven. He causes his sun to rise on the evil and the good, and sends rain on the righteous and the unrighteous.

John 8:3–11

The teachers of the law and the Pharisees brought in a woman caught in adultery. They made her stand before the group and said to Jesus, 'Teacher, this woman was caught in the act of adultery. In the Law Moses commanded us to stone such women. Now what do you say?' … he straightened up and said to them, 'If any one of you is without sin, let him be the first to throw a stone at her.' … At this, those who heard began to go away one at a time, the older ones first, until only Jesus was left, with the woman still standing there. Jesus straightened up and asked her, 'Woman, where are they? Has no-one condemned you?' 'No-one, sir,' she said. 'Then neither do I condemn you,' Jesus declared. Go now and leave your life of sin.

Forgiveness and love are at the centre of Jesus' teaching: 'Love your neighbour as yourself' (Matthew 22:39b). In the Lord's Prayer which Jesus taught to his disciples, Christians pray: 'Forgive us our sins, for we also forgive everyone who sins against us' (Luke 11:4a).

This suggests that if Christians wish to be forgiven by God, they should be prepared to forgive other people. This does not mean that a person who commits a wrong action should get away with it, but that if they repent (are truly sorry) they should be forgiven.

Reconciliation

In the Roman Catholic Church, a person can ask for forgiveness through the Sacrament of Reconciliation (Confession), where they tell a priest what they have done and the priest helps them to make amends for their actions through prayer and **repentance**.

This sacrament comes from the time when Jesus gave the power to his disciples to forgive sins on behalf of God:

> **John 20:21–23**
> *Again Jesus said, 'Peace be with you! As the Father has sent me, I am sending you.' And with that he breathed on them and said, 'Receive the Holy Spirit. If you forgive anyone his sins, they are forgiven; if you do not forgive them, they are not forgiven.'*

When they have made their confession the person may be asked to say prayers or do some community work as penance, then the priest says:

66 *God, the Father of mercies,*
through the death and resurrection of his Son
has reconciled the world to himself
and sent the Holy Spirit among us
for the forgiveness of sins;
through the ministry of the Church
may God give you pardon and peace,
and I absolve you from your sins
in the name of the Father, and of the Son,
and of the Holy Spirit.
(the penitent answers) Amen. **99**

For many Christians the central act of forgiveness and reconciliation is in the Sacrament of the **Eucharist**. Christians believe that God sent Jesus to be sacrificed on the cross in order to reconcile God with humanity. Humans are forgiven through the death and resurrection of Jesus, and this is remembered at the Eucharist.

> **Matthew 26:26–28**
> *While they were eating, Jesus took bread, gave thanks and broke it, and gave it to his disciples, saying, 'Take and eat; this is my body.'*
> *Then he took the cup, gave thanks and offered it to them, saying, 'Drink from it, all of you. This is my blood of the covenant, which is poured out for many for the forgiveness of sins.'*

REMEMBER THIS

Remember 'Love your neighbour as yourself' is one of the two Great Commandments given by Jesus. The first one is 'Love the Lord your God'.

ACTIVITIES

'Some sins can never be forgiven.' Do you agree? How might a Christian respond to this statement?

Remember and Reflect

The questions in this section are based on the work you have done throughout this Topic. Try to complete as many questions as you can.

The questions in set 1 are designed to test your factual recall and AO1 level skills (knowledge and understanding). The page numbers alongside the questions will help you to find information that might be useful for your answers. Use them to check against what you have written.

The questions in set 2 are more challenging, using AO2 level skills (use of evidence and reasoned argument to evaluate personal responses and differing viewpoints). Your answers many come from more than one part of the Topic.

AO1 Describe, explain and analyse, using knowledge and understanding

Find the answer on:

1 What is meant by
   a *prejudice*
   b *discrimination*
   c *equality?*

PAGE 153

2 Name three things for which people might be discriminated against.

PAGE 154

3 Explain what is meant by discrimination = power + prejudice.

PAGE 154

4 Give examples of two Biblical teachings about equality, one from the Old Testament and one from the New Testament.

PAGE 154, 155

5 What is meant by 'proselytising' and 'evangelising'?

PAGE 154, 155

6 Explain the traditional role of a missionary.

PAGE 158

7 Explain how missionaries work today.

PAGE 158, 159

8 What were the Crusades?

PAGE 158, 159

9 Why did the Spanish navy kill so many people in South America?

PAGE 156

10 What does the New Testament say about slavery?

PAGE 156

11 Explain what is meant by apartheid.

PAGE 156

12 Which Christian denomination supported apartheid?

PAGE 156

13 Who was Priscilla?

PAGE 157

14 Which famous American woman chaired the Committee which produced the United Nations Declaration of Human Rights?

PAGE 154

15 Which English cathedral is often associated with reconcilliation?

PAGE 160

Use evidence and reasoned argument to express and evaluate personal responses, informed insights, and differing viewpoints

1. 'It is not possible to treat everyone equally.' Do you agree with this statement? Explain your thinking on this issue.

2. Do you think that all churches should ordain women as priests? Construct a set of arguments for and against this statement.

3. What do you think a Christian would say to the following question: 'Why does the Church treat men and women differently?'

4. 'The existence of black churches shows that Christianity is still racist.' Do you agree with this statement? Explain your thinking on this issue.

5. 'All people are equal in the eyes of God and therefore there should be no leaders in church.' Do you agree with this statement? Explain your thinking on this issue.

6. 'All protest should be non-violent.' Construct a paragraph that a Christian might write in response to this statement.

7. 'The first two articles of the United Nations Declaration of Human Rights do not agree with Christian teaching.' Consider the arguments for and against this statement and weigh these up to come to a conclusion.

8. Copy and complete the table below to show how a Christian, a non-believer, and you would respond to the statements. (Remember: not all religious believers agree on everything, so try to reflect this in your answers.) Make sure you include reference to religious knowledge and give as many reasons for each view as possible.

Statement	What would a Christian say and why?	What would a non-believer say and why?	What would you say and why?
All people are equal			
All types of discrimination are wrong			
Christians should always be prepared to fight for equality			
Everyone is prejudiced and there is nothing anyone can do to change this			
All Christians should worship together			

Welcome to the Grade Studio

Grade Studio is here to help you improve your answers by working through typical questions you might find on an examination paper. For a full explanation of how this feature works and how exam questions are structured, see page 14. For a full explanation of Assessment Objectives and Levels of Response, see pages x–xi in the Introduction.

AO1 Question

Explain Christian teaching about whether men and women are equal. **[6 marks]**

Student's answer

Christians believe that God created men and women equal. It says in the Bible, 'male and female created he them'. Therefore they must be equal and should be able to do the same things.

Some Christians might also believe the story in the second creation account in Genesis, which says that Eve was made from Adam's rib. This may mean that women are inferior to men. The Bible seems to accept that women are not equal because St Paul said they are not allowed to speak in church. Their role is to be a wife and mother like Mary the Mother of Jesus.

Comments

The candidate has given a satisfactory answer to the question. There are two relevant points but neither is explained in any detail. In order to reach Level 3 the candidate needs to give more information and examples. The candidate could also use more technical terms from the specification to show the breadth of their knowledge and understanding.

Student's improved answer

Christians believe that God created men and women equal. It says in the Bible, 'male and female created he them'. Therefore they must be equal. Some Christians might also believe the story in the second creation account in Genesis, which says that Eve was made from Adam's rib. This may mean that women are inferior to men. The Bible seems to accept that women are not equal because St Paul said they are not allowed to speak in church. Their role is to be a wife and mother like Mary the Mother of Jesus.

Although in the past many people might have shared this view of women as being secondary to men, Christian views have changed over the last hundred years. Today most Christians would say that God made all people equal and that this includes men and women. Women now have the same rights as men and, in recent years, women have been able to become priests or ministers in many denominations of the Christian church. Therefore, women should be seen and treated as equal to men in society and everywhere else. The Roman Catholic church sees women and men as having different roles but as being equally important.

Comments

This is now a good answer to the question. The candidate has shown a clear understanding of the question. There is good description and explanation of a variety of different attitudes towards the equality of women, with good analysis. The information is presented clearly and there is good use of technical terms.

AO2 Question

'Men and women are not equal.' Discuss this statement. You should include different, supported points of view and a personal viewpoint. You must refer to Christianity in your answer. **[12 marks]**

Student's answer

Christians might say that, if God intended men and women equal, then he would have made them the same. But they are different and so they can't be equal. Some Christians might also say that God created women to be helpmates to men, and that they are made weaker because they don't have to work but have to give birth to babies and stay at home, while men have to work.

Comments

The candidate has given a limited answer to the question. There are two points but they both address the same issue and neither is expanded very far. In order to to reach Level 4 the candidate needs to give alternative viewpoints and also include a personal response.

Student's improved answer

Christians might say that, if God intended men and women equal, then he would have made them the same. But they are different and so they can't be equal. Some Christians might also say that God created women to be helpmates to men, and that they are made weaker because they don't have to work but just have to give birth to babies and stay at home, while men have to work.

Comments

This is now a good answer to the question. The candidate has shown a clear understanding of the question and has presented a range of views supported by evidence and argument. The answer explains Christian views, amongst others, and includes a personal viewpoint, which is also supported.

The majority of Christians and other people would disagree with this statement. Though it might appear from the Bible that women are inferior to men, many people would say that this simply reflects the time in which it was written. God created both sexes and everyone is equal before God. Some Christians would show how Jesus treated women as equals by speaking to them or mixing with them, which was unusual in his time. Others might say that if Jesus thought they were equal he would have had both men and women disciples. This is why some Christians such as Roman Catholics believe that men and women have very different roles to perform in life and in Christian worship. This does not mean 'they don't see them as equal, just different'. My personal opinion is that it is obvious that men and women are equal just by looking at how they work and what they do.

Nowadays both sexes are able to do the same things and there is no difference. If any religion teaches that they are not equal, then I believe that the religion is wrong.

These specimen answers provide an outline of how you could construct your response. Space does not allow us to give a full response. You will need to provide more detail in your actual exam responses.

Topic 12: Religion and the media

The Big Picture

In this Topic, you will be addressing Christian beliefs and teachings about:

- the relationship between the media and how they represent Christ and Christian beliefs
- the use of the media
- the concepts of censorship and freedom of speech.

You will also think about your own feelings and responses to these questions and issues.

DID YOU KNOW?

- The term 'media' refers to all the methods of mass communication. These include print, radio, television, art, music and all forms of communication technology.

- As the main religion practised in the UK, the media look to leading figures in Christianity to comment on social and ethical issues.

- Films about Christianity are seen as a good way to promote understanding of the faith.

- Radio and television programmes like *Thought for the Day* and *Songs of Praise* promote Christianity, while comedies like *Father Ted* and *The Vicar of Dibley* take a lighter view.

- Christians believe humans are made in the image of God, so anything that promotes the degradation of people is unacceptable.

KEY WORDS

allegories The symbolic expression of a deeper meaning through a story or scene acted out by human, animal, or mythical characters.

blasphemy To cause offence by comments about religious figures or religious ideas.

censorship To certify or to cut a piece of work in order to make sure that it does not cause offence.

freedom of speech The belief that people should have the right to express their own opinions as they wish.

homophobe Someone who shows an irrational hatred, disapproval, or fear of homosexuality, gay and lesbian people, or their culture.

media Methods of communication, for example television, radio, cinema, computers.

racist Someone who shows prejudice, discrimination or ill treatment against someone else because of their race.

sexist Someone who shows prejudice, stereotyping or discrimination, typically against women, on the basis of sex.

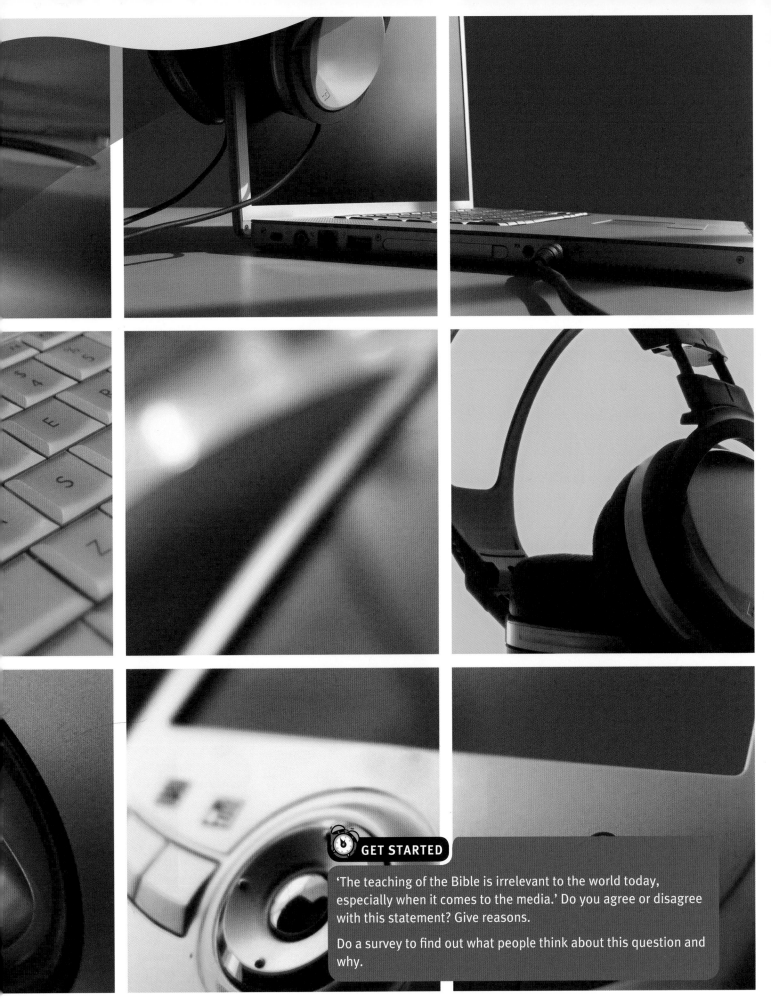

GET STARTED

'The teaching of the Bible is irrelevant to the world today, especially when it comes to the media.' Do you agree or disagree with this statement? Give reasons.

Do a survey to find out what people think about this question and why.

What are the different types of media?

The next two pages will help you to:

- examine different forms of media
- evaluate the influence of the media.

There are many different types of media.

Different forms of media

Media is defined as 'the means of mass communication, especially television, radio, and newspapers collectively'. Increasingly, it also refers to other ways in which we communicate or share information.

We live in a world saturated by information, by entertainment: we are in an age when more people can communicate with each other than ever before but is it always useful? We live in a world where hundreds of satellite channels can give us seemingly infinite choice. The Internet has opened up possibilities of communication which were impossible ten years ago.

In the last 150 years, the ways in which people communicate with each other have developed. Printing had developed in Europe in the 15th century and had enabled many to own books. By the Victorian period, most families in Britain had a family Bible.

AO1 skills ACTIVITIES

One form of media is the book. Working with a partner make a list of five books you admire. Why have you chosen the books you have? How similar or different are they? Why do you think that some books survive and are still important decades after they are written while others disappear quite quickly?

The development of the telephone, telegraph and the film had begun by the end of the 19th century. Radio and television were important methods of communication, with radio becoming important from the 1920s and television by the 1950s. By the 1980s, computer technology was developing. As the 1980s ended, new forms of communication and media were becoming increasingly important.

Technology such as the Internet, satellite television, the mobile phone, video and the DVD have enabled culture to spread and for ideas that were once the province of the few to be shared with the many. Cultures have increasingly intermingled. Much modern music is a hybrid of styles, reflecting many different cultures coming together.

How can the media be an influence?

The media can be a valuable place where injustice can be challenged. A programme like *Watchdog* has done a service, in that it exposes rogue businessmen who use dishonest or unsafe practices. Some of the political events have been exposed by the media, for example when *The Sunday Times* began to investigate why morning sickness pills called thamolide could lead to problems, it did a great service.

When journalists Bob Woodward and Carl Bernstein of *The Washington Post* exposed the involvement of President Richard Nixon in a political plot in 1972, which came to be known as the Watergate Scandal, they were helping to expose illegal behaviour. This led to a series of events which resulted in Nixon resigning his role as a result of his involvement in a cover up over the break in.

The media can be used to encourage people to reflect on the needs of others. In 1984, the Ethiopian famine was covered by *BBC News*. It led to a group of musicians led by Bob Geldof writing and recording the song, Band Aid's *Do They Know it's Christmas?* This led to a concert called Live Aid in 1985, the development of Comic Relief and in 2005 the Live 8 campaign was extensively covered in its attempts to get the richest nations to help others.

The power of adverts on television can be extremely strong: many children find it hard to resist the selling that goes on, especially in the round up to Christmas. As well as covering important events, television can often distort or make something seem important that is not vital. The reality television shows like *I'm a Celebrity Get Me Out of Here* or *Big Brother* or quiz programmes like *The Weakest Link* encourage us to be judgmental or delight in the belittling of others.

Some Christians are concerned that some forms of media such as television or the Internet can become very addictive and lead to people becoming less interested in doing other activities. They might point to the growth in obesity as an issue. Similarly, some Christians are unsure if their children should watch the television or use a computer without parental control.

RESEARCH NOTE

Find out what is meant by the 'God Slot'.

FOR DEBATE

How might the media be an influence for good and for bad?

AO2 skills ACTIVITIES

'Christians should realise that watching too much television will compromise their faith.' What do you think? What might Christians say? Show that you have thought about this from several different points of view and include Christian teachings and beliefs in your answer.

Portrayal of Christianity in the media

The next two pages will help you to:

- examine how Jesus and Christians are portrayed in the media
- examine how Christians have reacted to these depictions
- evaluate the portrayal of Jesus and Christianity in films.

Jesus Christ Superstar (1973).

Portrayal of Jesus in films

Jesus asked his disciples the question 'Who do people say the Son of Man is?' (Matthew 16:13b). It is a question that has gained a new importance as a consequence of the way Jesus has been seen in films and television. The development of cinema in the 20th century gave rise to new ways of depicting Jesus and Christianity. Films such as *From the Manger to the Cross* (1912) and *The Greatest Story Ever Told* (1965) had very few people objecting to the depiction of Jesus. Jesus was also shown in film versions of the novels *Ben-Hur* (1907, 1925 and 1959) and *The Robe* (1953), both of which were set in the time of Christ.

As cinema developed and society changed, the way in which Jesus was shown changed and reflected the way Christianity was being seen. In 1964 the Italian film director Pier Paolo Pasolini made a version of *The Gospel According to Matthew* in which Christ was seen as a Marxist-like revolutionary.

AO1 skills ACTIVITIES

How would you try to communicate the story of Jesus in a way that would be interesting to modern cinema goers? Work with a partner to come up with a few ideas which you can present to the class.

Stage musicals such as *Godspell* and *Jesus Christ Superstar* portrayed Jesus as a thought-provoking clown and as a man riddled with doubt. In 1988, Martin Scorcese's *The Last Temptation of Christ* caused controversy as it included a dream sequence in which Jesus had sexual intercourse with Mary Magdalene, which many Christians found objectionable.

There have been more conventional versions of the life of Jesus such as the television series *Jesus of Nazareth* (1977) and *The Passion* (2008). In 2000, the animated film *The Miracle Maker*, saw Jesus mainly through the eyes of a child he had cured by a miracle.

The film that has provoked most fierce argument was Mel Gibson's *The Passion of the Christ* (2004). The dialogue was in Aramaic, the language that Jesus may have spoken. The controversial element of the film (which led to it receiving an 18 certificate) was the use of bloody violence in the whipping and crucifying of Christ scenes. While Mel Gibson argued it was realistic, many people thought that these scenes were shot more like a horror film than a conventional Bible-based film.

How are Christians portrayed in the media?

One of the most famous fictional Christians in the media at the moment is probably Ned Flanders in *The Simpsons*. He is seen as rather silly, but frequently his depiction is quite sensitive.

Many Christians complain that when Christian characters appear in the media they are either silly or figures of fun or seen as extremists. Others say that on news and current affairs programmes, the producers quite often choose the most controversial person they can find who has faith rather than someone who is representative of faith.

In 2008, Channel 4 broadcast a programme called *Make me a Christian*. One of the Christian ministers involved, the Reverend Joanna Jepson, took legal action against Channel 4 because she felt that the programme had been edited in a way to distort what had happened and what she and others had said. The documentary series *The Monastery* made in 2005 won praise from Christians for its depiction of five men choosing to stay at Worth Abbey to find out what the monks believed and if it could be of use to them.

Films can be a very important way to explain faith. Many Christian organisations have tried to use film as a way to communicate the faith. The American Christian leader Billy Graham for a number of years encouraged the production of films, such as a version of *The Hiding Place* (1975), the story of the Dutch Christian Corrie ten Boom and her family helping Jews escape from the Holocaust. However, some Christians were critical of such films, feeling that although the cause was good, the production values and acting were not always of the highest standards.

Some Christians have sponsored films such as *The Chronicles of Narnia: The Lion, the Witch and the Wardrobe* (2005) by getting involved with established film producers. Others continue to develop their own films. A series of films called *Left Behind* (2000–08) have been distributed showing what one particular group of Christians believe will happen at the second coming of Jesus.

RESEARCH NOTE

Using the Internet, how many films about Jesus can you find?

FOR DEBATE

It is more important to have films which communicate religious beliefs than to worry about their quality. What do you think and why?

AO2 skills ACTIVITIES

'Christians cannot expect to be treated fairly in the media.' What do you think? What might a Christian say? Focusing on the depiction of Jesus and Christianity in films give reasons for your answers, showing that you have thought about several different points of view.

How do comics and books show religious and philosophical messages?

The next two pages will help you to:

- explain how comics and books focus on philosophical and religious messages
- examine how the media can be used to educate Christians and non-Christians
- evaluate how the television represents Christianity.

Comics and their values

Comics are a very important way for young people to relax. They often contain values and ideas that reflect the concerns of their creators.

Superheroes have often been seen as semi-religious figures. When the film *Superman Returns* came out in 2006, many critics pointed out the use of Christian imagery throughout the story where Superman almost seemed to be being presented as a Christ-like figure. The two people who created him were both Jewish, but did they consciously or unconsciously use some of the imagery of a Messiah that you might find in Christianity? They often represented the ideal human being, who would take a stand against the evil of their day.

In recent years, superheroes have been seen as less like miracle-working strong people but increasingly as people with problems or dealing with their own 'dark sides', their own tendency to be violent or selfish, such as in the film *The Dark Knight*, the film and graphic novel re-telling of the Batman story.

What about books and their messages?

Many authors such as G.K. Chesterton, Dorothy L. Sayers, T.S. Eliot, John Betjeman and Evelyn Waugh have written about their faith or found it influenced their writing. In the 1980s Susan Howatch began a series of very popular novels about Christians living in the 20th century called *The Starbridge Series*.

Perhaps the best known Christian writers were C.S. Lewis and J.R.R. Tolkien. Lewis created his famous books *The Chronicles of Narnia* (which includes *The Lion, the Witch and the Wardrobe*), in which he showed Jesus as a lion called Aslan. Lewis also wrote a science fiction trilogy about a Professor who visited planets and took on the abuse of science on earth.

AO1 skills **ACTIVITIES**

With a partner make a list of what is special and different about comics. Compare this with the rest of the class.

Tolkien, unlike Lewis, said that his books *The Hobbit* and *The Lord of the Rings* were not written to show Christian ideas. He rejected the idea that they were **allegories** (stories with hidden, deeper meanings). Yet it is very clear that in this make-believe world of elves and wizards, Tolkien's Christian point of view comes through.

More recently some Christians were unhappy with the success of the *Harry Potter* books because they considered that they promoted witchcraft which they believed to be the work of the Devil. Their author J.K. Rowling has acknowledged her debt to the work of Lewis and Tolkien. Other Christians have seen in the series a number of spiritual and moral points which, far from being against Christianity, have echoed Christian belief.

How can the media represent Christianity?

The media has had a very important role in communicating Christian faith. When the BBC was founded in 1922, it broadcast a daily service, which it still does to this day. There are dedicated slots for both Christians and others to speak about the issues of the day, in Radio 4's *Thought for the day* and *Pause for thought* on Radio 2. BBC television has had *Songs of Praise*, a programme dedicated to Christian music and worship, on Sundays for over fifty years. Many Christians feel that the media, be it television, radio or the newspapers can never fully explain and show their faith accurately and that it tends focus onto the odd or extreme aspects about faith.

The media does give both religious and non-religious people an opportunity to learn about the world, including issues about religious faith. Channel 4 showed an eight-part series in 2009 which told the story of Christianity from its beginnings and which was widely appreciated by Christians and non-Christians alike. Some Christians are using digital television stations to spread their messages, but other Christians are worried that these are normally run by narrow-minded people who perhaps do not show an accurate picture of what it is to be a Christian.

Although there are these serious-based programmes, many Christians are still concerned that in popular shows such as soaps or comedies, they are often presented in a less than flattering or accurate light.

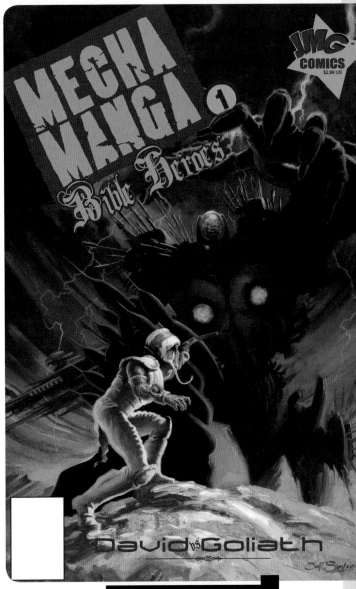

The cover of the first volume of the **Mecha Manga Bible Heroes.**

 **ACTIVITIES**

'Christians cannot expect an accurate depiction of their faith on television.' What do you think of this statement? What might Christians think? Give reasons for your answers, showing that you have thought about it from more than one point of view.

What are freedom of speech and censorship?

The next two pages will help you to:

- examine the concepts of censorship and freedom of speech
- evaluate the attitudes Christians have to freedom of speech
- examine beliefs and attitudes towards the portrayal of violence and sex.

What is censorship?

Censorship can be defined as 'suppressing or removing unacceptable parts of (a book, film, etc.)'. Censors are concerned with trying to assess the appropriate level of content for the audience of a film, a book etc. They have to make judgements about the content on such issues as sex, violence, **blasphemy** and horror. They have to be constantly reviewing their decision: what might have been acceptable at one time becomes totally unacceptable at another.

Jerry Springer: The Opera was a controversial stage musical which was broadcast on BBC 2 in January 2005. The organisation *Christian Voice* led protests against its transmission and over 55,000 people complained, especially about the depiction of Jesus in the second half of the programme, which it believed to be blasphemous. Attempts to prosecute the BBC failed. The BBC Director General Mark Thompson spoke in defence of the programme as did the show's star, David Soul. Both men were committed Christians and did not see anything in the piece that should upset believers.

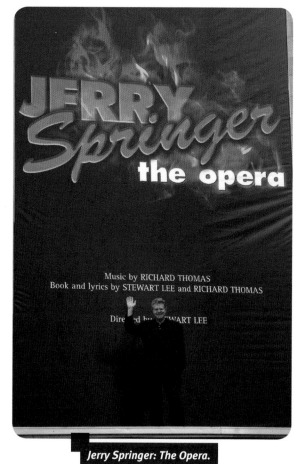

Jerry Springer: The Opera.

What is freedom of speech?

Freedom of speech is the belief that people should be entitled to freely express their ideas. In the 1930s, the Nazi regime of Germany eroded freedom of speech. Here is a poem by Martin Niemöller, a Christian pastor in Germany, about his reaction to this time:

> 66 *First they came for the Jews*
> *and I did not speak out –*
> *because I was not a Jew.*
> *Then they came for the Communists*
> *and I did not speak out –*
> *because I was not a communist.*
> *Then they came for the trade unionists*
> *and I did not speak out –*
> *because I was not a trade unionist.*
> *Then they came for me –*
> *And there was no one left*
> *to speak out for me.* 99

RESEARCH NOTE

Do some further research on Martin Niemöller and his poem *First they came*.

Do we have an automatic right to say what we think?

In Britain, there are laws designed to stop **racist**, **sexist** and **homophobic** abuse. It is, for example, illegal to address a public rally and encourage people to be use violence against a racial group. Trying to make laws can be controversial. One example, from 2006, is when the Government tried to introduce a *Racial and Religious Hatred Bill*, they found themselves under attack from a coalition of religious groups and comedians who felt the proposed law might limit their ability to make jokes about religious themes. Lawyers felt it would be difficult to enforce and politicians felt that there were enough existing laws to protect people. It was defeated.

Christians believe that you must speak responsibly. In his letter, James warns Christians of the dangers of abusing the gift of speech (see James 3:5–11).

What is a Christian response to free speech?

Some Christians say that free speech is not helpful, as it does not take into account that respect of others is more important than to say what you like.

Other Christians believe that they need to engage with the culture around them and not try to ignore or stop it. For example the Greenbelt Christian Arts Festival held each year in August also tries to look at a variety of opinions, many of which are not necessarily Christian, so that the people who attend the event can think through an issue. It invited the homosexual rights campaigner Peter Tatchell to talk about his work and his motivations, even though he is known for being critical of many Christians' negative attitudes to gay people.

Christianity and morality

Many Christians feel that the **media** should reflect the standard the early Christian leader Paul wrote about: 'Finally, brothers, whatever is true, whatever is noble, whatever is right, whatever is pure, whatever is lovely, whatever is admirable – if anything is excellent or praiseworthy – think about such things' (Philippians 4:8).

Many Christians think that by focusing on these qualities they are tapping into a general morality shared by all people. Other Christians point to the fact that this list includes the word 'true' – in other words, dramas or documentaries that responsibly show the bad side of life are not against the spirit of this passage. They believe that it is important to confront the evil in society and in the world, as the prophets of the Bible and Jesus himself challenged the lack of social justice or the treatment of the poor, who were powerless in their days.

Many Christians have been particularly upset by the way sex is shown in the media, for example, in soap operas and in the James Bond movies, sex can often be treated lightly and without respect for Christian teaching. Similarly, Christians might have concerns about bad language or blasphemy. Some have been worried by the use of occult-themed programmes and the messages they might be sending.

ACTIVITIES

Read James 3:5–11. Think carefully about what it says and then rewrite it in your own words so that its meaning is clear.

ACTIVITIES

'Christians should allow writers and artists their freedom to use their art as they like.' What do you think? What might Christians say? Show that you have thought about it from more than one point of view.

Remember and Reflect

The questions in this section are based on the work you have done throughout this Topic. Try to complete as many questions as you can.

The questions in set 1 are designed to test your factual recall and AO1 level skills (knowledge and understanding). The page numbers alongside the questions will help you to find information that might be useful for your answers. Use them to check against what you have written.

The questions in set 2 are more challenging, using AO2 level skills (use of evidence and reasoned argument to evaluate personal responses and differing viewpoints). Your answers many come from more than one part of the Topic.

AO1 Describe, explain and analyse, using knowledge and understanding

Find the answer on:

1 Explain what censorship and freedom of speech mean.	**PAGE 167, 174**
2 Give five examples of different types of media.	**PAGE 168, 169**
3 Outline three ways the media can influence people for good.	**PAGE 169**
4 Outline three ways in which the media can be a negative influence on people.	**PAGE 169**
5 Give two reasons for and two reasons against censorship.	**PAGE 174, 175**
6 Give two reasons for and against the freedom of speech.	**PAGE 174, 175**
7 Name five films which have portrayed Jesus.	**PAGE 170, 171**
8 Name five authors whose faith has influenced their writing.	**PAGE 172**
9 Explain the terms racist, sexist and homophobic.	**PAGE 167**
10 What is an allegory? Name a book which uses allegories.	**PAGE 173**
11 What is blasphemy?	**PAGE 174**
12 Who was Martin Niemöller?	**PAGE 174**
13 Why are some Christians unhappy with the Harry Potter books?	**PAGE 173**

AO2 Use evidence and reasoned argument to express and evaluate personal responses, informed insights, and differing viewpoints

1 Answer the following, giving as much detail as possible. You should give at least three reasons to support your response and also show that you have taken into account opposite opinions.
   - *Christians are always presented in a negative light on television.*
   - *Do you think Christian teaching contained in the Bible is relevant in today's world especially when it comes to the Media?*
   - *Do you think a Christian should be in favour of freedom of speech?*
   - *Christians should not be other people's censors.*

2 'We need a religious hatred law that protects all religious people.' What are the arguments for and against this? Refer to Christian teaching in your answers.

3 'Organisations like the BBC have a duty not to offend Christians.' What do you think? Give reasons for your answer and show that you have thought about it from several different points of view.

4 'Films are not able to show Christian ideas, so Christians should try other forms of the media.' Give reasons for your answer and show that you have thought about it from several different points of view.

5 Watch one of the soap operas on television for a week and using this form, note down every time that one of the commandments below is broken.

The Ten Commandments	Example of how this rule was broken in a soap opera
You shall have no other gods before me.	
You shall not make for yourself an idol in the form of anything in heaven above or on the earth beneath or in the waters below.	
You shall not misuse the name of the Lord your God.	
Remember the Sabbath day by keeping it holy.	
Honour your father and your mother	
You shall not murder.	
You shall not commit adultery.	
You shall not steal.	
You shall not give false testimony against your neighbour.	
You shall not covet.	

Welcome to the Grade Studio

Grade Studio is here to help you improve your answers by working through typical questions you might find on an examination paper. For a full explanation of how this feature works and how exam questions are structured, see page 14. For a full explanation of Assessment Objectives and Levels of Response, see pages x–xi in the Introduction.

AO1 Question

Explain Christian attitudes towards the portrayal of violence in the media.

[6 marks]

Student's answer

Christians believe that violence is wrong and should not be shown in the media because it goes against the Ten Commandments to harm people or to kill them. And if it is shown in the media it suggests people should enjoy it.

Some Christians might also believe that portraying violence in the media might encourage people to be more violent because they see their heroes in the media being violent and will want to follow their role model.

Comments

The candidate has given a satisfactory answer to the question. There are two relevant points but only one of them really relates to Christianity. In order to reach Level 3 the candidate needs to give more information and examples. The candidate could also use more technical terms from the specification to show the breadth of their knowledge and understanding.

Student's improved answer

Christians believe that violence is wrong and should not be shown in the media because it goes against the Ten Commandments to harm people or to kill them. And if it is shown in the media it suggests people should enjoy it.

Some Christians might also believe that portraying violence in the media might encourage people to be more violent because they see their heroes in the media being violent and will want to follow their role model.

Some people might say that showing violence just to make the programme more exciting is never justified because it plays to an unhealthy desire to enjoy watching people suffer. Other Christians accept that sometimes it is necessary to portray violence in order to explain the story, for example, the whipping of Jesus in the Passion of the Christ. If the story is a violent one, there is bound to be violence, but it should be handled sensitively and not glorified.

Many Christians might say that the portrayal of violence is something that has to be judged on a case-by-case basis rather than by a single rule that it is right or wrong.

Comments

This is now a good answer to the question. The candidate has shown a clear understanding of the question. There is good description and explanation of a variety of different responses to the portrayal of violence. The candidate has shown some analysis in dealing with the question. The information is presented clearly and there is good use of technical terms.

AO2 Question

'People should never be allowed to make fun of religion in the media.' Discuss this statement. You should include different, supported points of view and a personal viewpoint. You must refer to Christianity in your answer. **[12 marks]**

Student's answer

Some Christians might say that it is always wrong to make fun of religion in the media, because religion is the most important aspect of their lives and it should be treated seriously so their feelings are not hurt.

Some Christians might also say that no one would like fun to be made of their religion or their personal beliefs, so why should people make fun of Christianity? The people who run the media should only do what they would like others to do to them.

Comments

The candidate has given a limited answer to the question. There are two relevant points but they both address the same point of view and neither is expanded. In order to reach Level 4 the candidate needs to give alternative viewpoints and also include a personal response.

Student's improved answer

Some Christians might say that it is always wrong to make fun of religion in the media, because religion is the most important aspect of their lives and it should be treated seriously so their feelings are not hurt.

Some Christians might also say that no one would like fun to be made of their religion or their personal beliefs, so why should people make fun of Christianity? The people who run the media should only do what they would like others to do to them.

Comments

This is now a good answer to the question. The candidate has shown a clear understanding of the question and has presented a range of views supported by evidence and argument. The answer explains Christian views, amongst others, and includes a personal viewpoint, which is also supported.

Some people, on the other hand, might say that it depends on what is meant by 'fun'. Humour is part of everyday life and, because people who follow a religion are also human, there may be occasions when humour is not hurtful, but just a joke that people can share. Some may say that making fun of individual people and what they do is fine but that this does not include actually making fun of their religion. Others might say that it is acceptable to make fun of how people practise their religion, but God or religious figures such as Jesus are too sacred for jokes to be made at their expense. This could be like blasphemy and would anger God. God deserves respect and making fun of him is disrespectful. I think that there are occasions when jokes about religion can be funny.

However, I think this must be done with respect and should not ever be done with the intention of offending people. We should always think how we would feel before we make fun of people or their beliefs.

These specimen answers provide an outline of how you could construct your response. Space does not allow us to give a full response. You will need to provide more detail in your actual exam responses.

ExamCafé

Welcome to Exam Café

Now you have finished the course/Topic, it is time to revise and prepare for the examination. A key to any exam is the revision and preparation leading up to it. The key to good revision is to 'work smart'. This section will guide you to know what is needed for success and, just as important, what is not. So don't panic! Think positive. GCSE is about what you *can* do, not what you can't.

Key points to note at this stage

1 Your revision will need to focus on producing the best possible answer. Remember the AO1 and AO2 assessment objectives. Each of these objectives is worth 50 per cent of the total mark.

2 You also need to know that the exam questions on the paper are designed to test your performance with both AO1 and AO2 objectives. Each question will be made up of five parts:

- Four AO1 parts, of which three check your knowledge and one tests your understanding and analysis.

- One question testing AO2 – your ability to consider different points of view on a particular issue and how much you can express your own points of view with relevant evidence and argument.

Once you understand what is needed, it will be time to turn to your revision programme.

How to get started

An important key to success with any exam is the preparation beforehand. While few people enjoy the process of revision, it is something that is vital for success. Your class teacher will also discuss revision with you. Below are some suggestions and ideas that can be employed:

1 It is vital to revise in plenty of time before the exam. Do not leave everything to the last minute.

2 Design a revision timetable and be realistic about what can be achieved.

3 Revision is a personal matter and we all learn in different ways. Remember that many revision skills can be transferred between different subjects.

4 These are some suggested revision techniques:

- Create summary cards for each topic – a maximum of 5–10 bullet points on each card.

- Create lists of key words and terms. Ask somebody to test you on them or hang them around the house.

- Create a mind map to summarise a major topic.

- Design cards with a word or idea on one side and a question/ definition or answer on the other. These allow you to be tested by family members or friends who may not have much subject knowledge.

- Create an A–Z list on a certain topic. This involves writing the 26 letters of the alphabet down the side of a page and then having to write a key word or teaching connected to that topic for each letter of the alphabet.

- Remember that religious teachings do not have to be learned word-for-word. It is acceptable to paraphrase them.

5 Break your revision sessions of 5–10 minutes to start with (this can be increased as you become much better at it). Give yourself a short break (of about 5 minutes) and then go back to revising. Remember that spending time revising when nothing is going in is as bad as doing no revision at all.

6 Try answering questions on past papers then marking them with the mark scheme yourself. Alternatively, you can write your own questions and develop your own mark scheme. Answer the questions and use the levels of response to mark them.

7 Finally, remember that if you go into revision with a negative attitude you are ultimately going to make it much tougher on yourself.

ExamCafé

Revision
Common errors and mistakes

So the day of the exam has arrived. Remember that you are not the first to sit exams and you will not be the last. However, learn from the experience of others and do not fall into any of the following exam traps:

Misreading the question: Take a minute and read the question carefully. Surprisingly a large number of candidates do not read the questions properly. They simply see a word or miss a point and feel they have to start writing. No matter how good your answer is, if it does not answer the question it will not gain you any marks.

Wasting valuable time: The exam is a race against the clock. Match the length of your response to the number of marks being awarded. A one-mark question can be answered with a single word or a sentence and not a paragraph.

Disorganised waffle: Written answers, especially AO2 style answers, require you to plan your answer thoughtfully. It requires a range of viewpoints including religious responses and your own views. Be careful and do not let your own views take over.

Poor selection of knowledge: Choose good examples that help you to develop and explain your ideas. For example if a question asks you to explain why it is important for Christians to read the Bible don't just answer 'because their religion requires it'.

It is Religious Studies after all: Remember that the subject is Religious Studies and you will be tested on your knowledge and understanding of religion and its impact on the lives of individuals and communities. Make sure your answers contain relevant religious ideas.

Know the exam paper: Make sure that you fully understand the layout and instructions for the exam paper. In particular focus on which questions you must do and how many questions you are required to do.

Revision checklist

The details of the course are known as the Specification. It is broken down into the Topics listed below. There is a summary of the key areas within each Topic that you need to know about.

TOPIC 7 RELIGION AND HUMAN RELATIONSHIPS

For this Topic you must:
- know the meaning of the technical terms in the specification so that you can answer factual questions such as 'What is meant by contraception?'
- know and understand the roles of men and women in a Christian family and in the Church family
- know and understand how marriage ceremonies reflect Christian teaching and also be able to explain attitudes towards civil partnerships
- be able to explain different Christian attitudes towards divorce, re-marriage after divorce and contraception.

TOPIC 8 RELIGION AND MEDICAL ETHICS

For this Topic you must:

- know and understand Christian teachings about the sanctity of life and how this belief is reflected in the issues in this Topic
- be able to explain different Christian attitudes towards issues of abortion, fertility treatment, cloning, euthanasia, suicide and the use of animals in medical research.

TOPIC 9 RELIGION, POVERTY AND WEALTH

For this Topic you must:

- focus on Christian understandings of the causes of hunger, poverty and disease
- be able to explain Christian responses to these issues, including giving money to charity as well as practical responses
- know Christian teachings about the use of money and ways in which it should not be used, for example gambling or lending at interest
- be able to explain what is meant by 'moral' and 'immoral', and what Christians might consider moral and immoral occupations.

TOPIC 10 RELIGION, PEACE AND JUSTICE

For this Topic you must:

- be able to give a detailed explanation of the Just War theory and Christian attitudes towards war
- explain Christian approaches to the use of violence and different attitudes towards pacifism
- understand the concept of justice and punishment
- be able to explain the aims of punishment and religious responses to capital punishment
- understand Christian responses to the treatment of criminals
- be able to explain Christian beliefs about social justice and injustice.

TOPIC 11 RELIGION AND EQUALITY

For this Topic you must:

- be able to explain Christian teaching about equality
- be able to explain Christian attitudes towards racism and gender issues
- show understanding of Christian attitudes towards other religions, including beliefs about spreading the teachings of Christianity and conversion
- be able to explain the words 'forgiveness' and 'reconciliation', and explain Christian beliefs about these.

TOPIC 12 RELIGION AND THE MEDIA

For this Topic you must:

- know about different types of media and be able to explain their influence
- be able to explain Christian attitudes towards the media and the way in which religious figures may be portrayed in the media
- be able to consider the use which Christianity can make of the media
- be able to explain the issues that are raised by the concepts of censorship and freedom of speech.

Exam**Café**

Exam preparation

Sample student answer

Now you have done some serious revision it is time to see what sort of responses you will need to produce to build the best answers. Here are some examples of responses with comments to show you what is good about them and how they could be improved.

Remember examiners will use levels of response for part d, which is AO1, and part e, which is AO2. For parts a, b and c, responses will be point marked. This means that if there is one mark allocated for the question, only one point is expected, if two marks are allocated, then two points are expected and so on. Part a is worth one mark, b two marks and c three marks.

AO1 a–c

Here are some AO1 point-marked questions and example responses from Topic 7: Religion and human relationships.

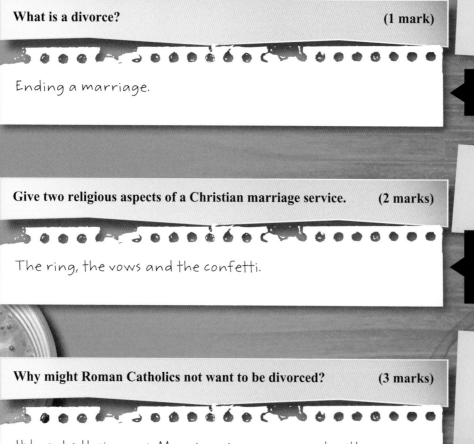

What is a divorce? (1 mark)

Ending a marriage.

> 'What is?' just means describe something – in this case, divorce.

Comment
Correct.

Give two religious aspects of a Christian marriage service. (2 marks)

The ring, the vows and the confetti.

> Check that you write about 'religious' aspects.

Comment
Responses 1 and 2 are correct, but response 3 is not a religious aspect.

Why might Roman Catholics not want to be divorced? (3 marks)

It breaks their vows. Marriage is a sacrament with promises made to God which cannot be broken. They will probably not be able to be re-married in church.

> Here, although there is only one-mark per point, you will need to be precise and concise in your response.

Comment
Three good reasons given.

AO1 Part d questions

Some AO1 answers are marked in levels of response. These are the part d of the questions and are worth six marks each. However, just because they are worth six marks it does not mean that you will need to produce six short points or develop three points in the answer. Instead you will need to show a level of understanding. The higher the level then the higher the level of understanding required. This could be done by referring to several points and expanding each a little, or by developing one or two points in greater detail. Here are some AO1 questions and example responses from Topic 8 : Religion and medical ethics.

> **Explain how Christians might respond to someone who wants to commit suicide.**
> (6 marks)

When answering this question, ask yourself the question 'why?' as soon as you have written down a reason. There are different levels of explanation, and the examiner is looking for depth not for a superficial level.

Response 1

Christians might say that it is wrong to commit suicide because it is killing, which is against the Ten Commandments. They might say that only God has the right to take life. They might try to cheer the person up by talking to them.

Comment
This is satisfactory response, reaching Level 2. The information given is relevant, and accurate reasons have been chosen. However, the response is not well developed and is essentially one-sided, giving only one explanation.

Response 2

Christians might say that it is wrong to commit suicide because it is murder, which is against the Ten Commandments. They might say that only God has the right to give life and to take it away.

Some Christians might try to talk the person out of it by showing them how much God loves them.

They may also persuade them to speak to an organisation like the Samaritans who help people in these situations. Also, they might show people how much they are loved and that there are still good things in life.

Comment
This is a good response. It contains much of the satisfactory response but it is much more developed. The reasons for different views are explained. This response would reach Level 3.

ExamCafé

Exam preparation

Sample student answer

AO2

Part e of each question in the exam will involve an AO2 question asking you to explain different points of view about a particular issue. It also gives you an opportunity to present your own personal viewpoint. However, please remember that all viewpoints on a particular issue must be backed up with good evidence, argument and reasoning. Part e of each question is worth 12 marks, or 50 per cent of the total, so it is important to think carefully about how you are going to tackle these questions.

Planning an AO2 answer

These questions want different points of view about a particular issue. Your answer could therefore be structured in the following way:

Paragraph 1: Explain a view that will *agree* with the statement in the question. Offer evidence, beliefs and teachings to back up the point of view.

Paragraph 2: Explain a *different* view from what the statement is suggesting. Again you need to offer evidence, beliefs and teachings to back up your point of view.

Paragraph 3: Include your own personal viewpoint about the issue raised. Again you need to offer evidence, belief and arguments to support your point of view. It does not matter which point of view you take, there is no right or wrong answer. Instead you will need to show your ability to reason and argue. If you really do not have a strong point of view on this issue just simply go for the viewpoint that you can best argue.

Here is an AO2 question and some example responses from Topic 11: Religion and equality.

> 'Christians should try to convert everyone to their religion.' (12 marks)

Response 1

Christians believe that it is their duty to make everyone join their religion so that they can go to heaven. Some people might say that this is wrong and people should be left to decide their religion for themselves.

Comment
This is Level 1. Two relevant viewpoints are stated but there is little support to back them up. This is a simplistic response and shows limited understanding of the question. There is no use of technical terms.

Response 2

Christians believe that it is their duty to make everyone join their religion so that they can go to heaven. This is because Christianity is a proselytising religion and 'gospels' are the 'good news' which they have to spread.

Some people might say that this is wrong and people should be left to decide their religion for themselves. It is wrong to try to persuade someone to join your religion just because you believe in it.

Response 3

Christians believe that it is part of their duty as followers of Jesus to make everyone join their religion so that they can go to heaven. This is because Christianity is a proselytising religion and 'gospels' are the 'good news' which they have to spread. They also believe that becoming a Christian is the only way in which people can reach heaven and the presence of God.

Some people might say that this is wrong and people should be left to decide their religion for themselves. It is wrong to try to persuade someone to join your religion just because you believe in it. Religion is a personal thing and no one should try to force you into it.

Others may think that everyone can listen to whatever they like and can then make their own decisions. My opinion is that it is very difficult for Christians not to try to persuade people to join their religion.

Response 4

Christians believe that it is part of their duty as followers of Jesus to make everyone join their religion so that they can go to heaven. This is because Christianity is a proselytising religion and 'gospels' are the 'good news' that they have to spread. They also believe that becoming a Christian is the only way in which people can reach heaven and the presence of God.

Some people might say that this is wrong and people should be left to decide their religion for themselves. It is wrong to try to persuade someone to join your religion just because you believe in it. Religion is a personal thing and no one should try to force you into it.

Others may think that everyone can listen to whatever they like and can then make their own decisions. It is no different to advertising anything else and it is up to people to decide whether to respond or not. Christians believe it is part of their religious duty. Jesus preached the good news and they have to do the same.

However, I do not like people knocking on my door trying to persuade me to join their faith and I think it should be left to individuals to come to their own decisions.

Comment
This is a Level 2. This is better answer as it explains to the examiner what the candidate understands the question to be about. However, although two viewpoints are stated and slightly developed, the response is still rather limited.

Comment
This is a satisfactory response and meets the criteria for Level 3. It is reasonably well organised and contains some significant views that are explained well and have evidence to justify them. There is a balance of views. There is good use of technical terms. However, there is no argument in support of the personal opinion and this limits the response to Level 3.

Comment
The personal response presents a new view and comes to a conclusion. The candidate has grasped the significance of the issue. The personal view is backed up by evidence. There is good accurate use of specialist terms and the response is reasonably well organised. This will take the response to Level 4.

ExamCafé

Exam preparation
Understanding exam language

Examiners try to keep questions short and clear. To do this they use special trigger words to hint at how you should respond to the questions. Below is a list of common trigger words. You should familiarise yourself with these words:

State	Usually used in AO1 questions worth 1–3 marks. This means 'write down a fact about something', for example *State the Just War theory*.
Give	This is used instead of 'state' and requires the same sort of response.
List	This is used instead of 'give' or 'state' and requires the same sort of response.
Describe	This is used in AO1 questions and means 'tell the examiner factual information about the item or idea'. An example is *Describe what is meant by euthanasia,* which means 'write down factual information about euthanasia'.
Give an account of	This is asking for the same sort of response as 'describe', for example *Give an account of the key Christian beliefs about the sanctity of life.*
Explain	This means show that you understand something, for example *Explain Christian attitudes to the use of animals in medical research*. An 'explain' response will include some knowledge, but the best responses will give a range of ideas and reasons.
Why	This word is used as shorthand for 'explain'. Substitute the word 'explain' and you will see what to do, for example *Why are there different Christian attitudes towards issues of abortion?* is the same as *Explain different Christian attitudes towards issues of abortion.*
How	This can be used to ask you for factual information, for example *How do marriage ceremonies reflect Christian teaching?* It can also be used for questions that are asking for understanding where there is a mixture of fact and understanding required, for example *How do Christians show compassion?*
Important	This word is used frequently in AO1 part d questions and it indicates that you say why Christians should or should not do/believe something. An example is *Explain why marriage is important to Christians*, which means, *Give reasons to explain why marriage is thought of in a special way in Christianity.*

Exam Tips
Planning and structuring an answer

In the Grade Studios you have been shown how to build levels of response. This is really important for the AO1 responses to part d worth six marks and the AO2 responses to part e worth 12 marks. In each case follow this structure:

- Check you really know what the question is asking. In the AO2 questions work out the key word or words in the statement, for example *Every woman has the right to have a baby. Discuss this statement.* The key phrase here is *Discuss this statement.* If the answer does not deal with this, then it will be awarded a low mark.
- Make a note of key points to include all AO1 responses and use a diagram to note down viewpoints for AO2.
- Begin your answer with a brief mention of what the question is asking you to do.
- Write clearly and concisely. DON'T WAFFLE.
- Reach a conclusion at the end of your answer. In the case of an AO1 answer this could be a brief summary sentence, for example *This shows why compassion is important to many Christians.* In the case of an AO2 answer the conclusion should include a **personal view** (with supporting reasons/argument) and a **brief summing up** of the different views you have expressed.
- Leave a gap of a few lines between each answer. This is in case you wish to add further ideas/information later (if you don't, there is no need to worry).
- If you have any time left at the end of your exam use it constructively. Check your answer makes sense. Check your answer is responding to the question set. Check your use of English, grammar and spelling. Check you have answered the required number of questions. **Remember when you hand in your answer paper at the end of the exam it is probably the last time you will ever see it. Make sure it is your best possible effort.**

Glossary

Abortion: Deliberate termination of pregnancy by removal and destruction of the foetus.

Adultery: A sexual relationship between a married person and someone to whom they are not married.

Allegories: The symbolic expression of a deeper meaning through a story or scene acted out by human, animal, or mythical characters.

Annulment: A marriage terminated by the Church because it was not valid.

Apostles' Creed: An early statement of Christian belief.

Authority: The idea that something has power over or can influence people in some way.

Big Bang: A scientific theory that a cosmic explosion caused the world to exist.

Blasphemy: To cause offence by comments about religious figures or religious ideas.

Capital punishment: Executing a criminal convicted of murder and other crimes.

Censorship: To certify or to cut a piece of work in order to make sure that it does not cause offence.

Charity: To give help or money to those in need.

Christian: A believer in and follower of Jesus.

Civil partnership: Legal recognition of a same-sex relationship with a registry office ceremony.

Clone: An individual organism or cell produced asexually from one ancestor to which they are genetically identical.

Commitment: A bond between a couple.

Committal: The actions that take place when a body is buried or cremated.

Compassion: Sympathy and concern for others.

Conscience: An inner voice or feeling giving guidance on the rightness or wrongness of behaviour.

Conscientious objector: Someone who refuses to fight in a war on the basis of conscience.

Conversion: A form of religious experience, usually to someone who afterwards changes their beliefs or behaviour.

Cosmological argument: The argument that there must be a 'first cause' and that this was God.

Covenant: A special promise or agreement between God and humans.

Creation: The act of creating something or the thing that is made in the Bible, the making of the world by God.

Creationists/Literalists: A name given to Christians who interpret the Bible literally and accept every word of the Genesis creation story as literally true.

Crucifix: Cross with the representation of Jesus on it, often a symbol of Christianity found in holy buildings or worn by many Christians on a necklace.

Day of Judgement: The day when God will judge everyone according to actions and faith on earth.

Denomination: A branch of Christianity; different types of Christians.

Discrimination: Unjust or prejudicial treatment because of race, age, gender or disability.

Divorce: The legal ending of a marriage.

Dominion: The idea that humans have control over or responsibility for the earth.

Ecumenical: Different Christian denominations working together.

Equality: Treating people as equals regardless of gender, race or religious beliefs.

Eucharist: The Christian ceremony commemorating the Last Supper, in which bread and wine are consecrated and consumed. Also known as the Mass or Holy Communion.

Eulogy: The speech or talk given at a funeral about the person who has died.

Euthanasia: When someone is helped to die without pain before they would have died naturally.

Evangelism: Persuading others to share your faith.

Evolution: The way in which animals and plants adapt to their surroundings – the survival of the fittest.

Ex nihilo: A Latin term relating to the creation story meaning the universe was created out of nothing.

Fasting: To go without food or something else chosen by an individual; in religion it is to empathise with others and try to get closer to God.

Father: One person of the threefold nature of God.

Forgiveness: Forgiving someone for something they have done wrong.

Free will: The belief that God created humans with the ability to make moral choices.

Freedom of speech: The belief that people should have the right to express their own opinions as they wish.

Funeral: The ceremony or service that occurs after someone has died.

Genesis: The first book of the Bible which contains the stories of creation.

Genetic engineering: The deliberate modification of the characteristics of an organism by manipulating its genetic material.

Golden rule: Jesus' teaching the people that they should treat others as they wish to be treated themselves.

Heaven: A Christian idea of paradise where the soul goes after death if it is free from sin to have eternal life with God.

Hell: A place that some Christians believe is a punishment after death for those souls that are not free from sin; it is often referred to as a place of torment or suffering without God.

Holy Spirit: One person of the threefold nature of God.

Homophobe: Someone who shows an irrational hatred, disapproval, or fear of homosexuality, gay and lesbian people, or their culture.

Humanity: Caring and showing kindness to others, often a term used for all humans.

Icons: Images or pictures which are used to aid focus and concentration in prayer.

Immoral: Not conforming to accepted standards of behaviour.

Incarnate: The doctrine that God took human form in Jesus.

Incarnation: God in human form as Jesus on earth.

Job: Biblical character whose faith is tested.

Judge: The Christian idea of God acting as a judge to determine whether a person goes to Heaven or Hell after death.

Just War theory: The belief that wars can be morally justified if they follow certain criteria.

Justice: Fairness in society and the world.

LEDC: Less economically developed country.

Lord's Prayer: Probably the most well-known prayer in Christianity, taught by Jesus to his followers.

MEDC: More economically developed country.

Media: Methods of communication, for example television, radio, cinema, computers.

Medical ethics: Questions of morality that are raised by medical situations.

Meditation: An idea connected to prayer and worship where an individual is occupied in thought and reflects deeply on spiritual matters or may concentrate on an idea or object.

Miracle: Something that is amazing and appears to defy the laws of nature, usually attributed to God.

Monotheism: Belief in one God.

Moral: Conforming to accepted standards of behaviour.

Moral evil: Evil and suffering caused by people.

Mysticism: A form of religious experience where the believer appears unaware of anything except their experience, feelings of unity and peace may be experienced.

Natural evil: Evil and suffering caused by natural events such as earthquakes.

Non-literalist: A name given to a Christian who interprets the Bible as more of a story than literalists and believes it contains important truths but is not a factual account.

Nuclear pacifism: Belief that the use of nuclear weapons can never be justified.

Numinous: Having a sense of being in the presence of the divine.

Omnipotent: Powerful, able to do anything.

Omnipresence: A characteristic of God used to explain that he is everywhere.

Omniscience: A characteristic of God used to describe him as all-knowing.

Omniscient: All-knowing.

Ontological argument: The argument based on the idea that God is greater than anything else people can think of.

Original Sin: The sin which was brought into the world at the Fall and which Christianity teaches everyone is born with.

Pacifism: The belief that peace should be the central value that people pursue.

Philanthropist: Someone who donates money, goods, services or time to help a cause which benefits society.

Prayer: Communication with God, either individually and privately or communally with others.

Prejudice: Making judgements not based on reason or actual experience.

Pre-marital sex: Having a sexual relationship before marriage.

Promiscuity: Having many sexual partners without commitment.

Proportionality: The belief that force can only be met with equal force.

Proselytising: Trying to convert people from their religion to yours.

Purgatory: In some Christian traditions, a condition or state in which good souls receive spiritual cleansing after death, in preparation for Heaven.

Quaker: A member of the Christian denomination also known as the Religious Society of Friends.

Racism: Prejudice, discrimination or ill treatment against someone because of their race.

Racist: Someone who shows prejudice, discrimination or ill treatment against someone else because of their race.

Reconciliation: Restoring friendly relations.

Redemption: The idea that sins can be forgiven and a person can be redeemed. Jesus is often referred to by Christians as the Redeemer as he died for the sins of the whole world.

Religious experience: An experience of God.

Re-marriage: Marrying again after divorce.

Repentance: Sincere regret or remorse for one's actions.

Resurrection: The rising from the dead of Jesus Christ on the third day after the crucifixion.

Revelation: The method through which something is revealed that was previously hidden; in a Christian sense it refers to believers gaining a better understanding of God as he is revealed to them.

Revenge: Seeking to repay a wrong by getting recompense.

Ritual: Order and set approach to worship, where the same actions may be performed.

Sacrament: A special action which brings Christians closer to God.

Sacred/sanctity: Holy, having something of God or the divine.

Sacrifice: Giving up life for God.

Salvation: Jesus came to earth to save people from their sins and achieved salvation through his sacrifice in death on the cross.

Sanctity of life: The belief that all life is given by God and is therefore sacred.

Sermon: A talk given by a minister which highlights an important issue or topic.

Sexism: Prejudice, stereotyping or discrimination, typically against women, on the basis of sex.

Sexist: Someone who shows prejudice, stereotyping or discrimination, typically against women, on the basis of sex.

Sin: An act which goes against God's will.

Social injustice: Where people may be denied rights as a consequence of poverty or discrimination.

Social justice: The belief that people should be treated fairly and with respect in a society.

Son: One person of the threefold nature of God.

Soul: Christians believe the soul is a non-physical and immortal part of the body that continues after death and is the connection with God.

Stewardship: The God-given right or responsibility to care for and manage the world.

Suicide: Deliberately ending one's own life.

Symbol: A picture or image that represents something else, it usually has a deeper or more significant meaning.

Teleological argument: The argument that the world is so complex that it must have had a designer and the designer must have been God.

The Devil/Satan: A supernatural evil power.

The Fall: The disobedience of Adam and Eve resulting in their expulsion from Eden.

Theodicies: Arguments justifying why there is evil in the world if God is good.

Tithe: The Christian act of giving a tenth of your income to charity.

Trade restrictions: Restrictions made by one country about the amounts and types of goods it will allow into the country from other countries.

Trinity: The Christian belief that God is three separate persons within One – Father, Son and Holy Spirit.

Violence: The use of physical force, with the intention to harm.

Vows: Sacred promises a couple make at their marriage.

Worship: A way of honouring or respecting God with great devotion.

Index